1

Introduction

Jenny smiles, her eyes filling with tears. Yes, she says, it does hurt, being treated like that – him making jokes and turning her friends against her. After going out with him for eight months she'd thought she could trust him.

We talk more about her boyfriend and about the things he's done. Then I ask about her family. She says that her dad left when she was two. All she knows about him is that he used to hit her mum and now her mum won't talk about it. Jenny can't decide what to think. She longs to know whether her dad still thinks about her the way she thinks about him. She wonders whether he's changed and whether, if he has a new wife, he hits her.

This book is about boyfriends and girlfriends – getting them, keeping them and moving on from them. Young people put enormous energy into these processes. They worry, they hope, they conspire and they cry because, in a sense, having a boyfriend or girlfriend is about much more than just having a boyfriend or girlfriend. This book is also about the internal, unconscious conflicts which boyfriends and girlfriends evoke in young people and – sometimes – resolve.

She hasn't seen him since she was two but Jenny's father still matters because he was supposed to be loyal. He was supposed to love her. Now she's discovered that the boy she was going out with for eight months isn't loyal and probably doesn't love her either. She's left wondering whether to keep hoping that she'll find someone who'll love her the way she's always longed to be loved; whether there are nice boys out there and whether, one day, she might just find one, even though she's never found the father who left all those years ago and who's never come back.

As a counsellor working with young people, I hear about all sorts of boyfriends and girlfriends – the lack of them, the betrayals by them, the break-ups with them, the fair and unfair things they do. Many of them are described in this book. They're loved and hated, idealised and demonised by the young people talking to me. But young people describe *so much* of their experience of the world in these terms. In talking about a wonderful boyfriend or woeful girlfriend, we'll inevitably be talking about other loves and hates; about parents like Jenny's father; about friends and enemies; about loneliness, intimacy, trust, shame and all sorts of other, underlying anxieties evoked by whoever happens to be the focus of our conversation.

I think we overlook the developmental importance of having a boyfriend or girlfriend. We assume it's a private matter, and most young people will readily agree with this for fear of being exposed or ridiculed. So we take our cue from them and don't interfere, complaining privately that they're growing up too fast, that their hormones are out of control, that they're obsessed with sex, that they spend their lives on the phone, that they don't know the meaning of love, that romance is dead... Ah well, we conclude, they'll just have to learn the hard way!

We leave them to get on with it. And they get hurt. They get stuck. They get drunk and fight and write poems and threaten to kill themselves. I'm not suggesting that parents or professionals should go barging into young people's lives without permission – privacy is a delicate matter – but I think it's important to be more than just available in principle. This book is about deliberately asking questions and then trying to understand the meaning of the defensive or desperate, spoken or unspoken answers which come back.

These answers are likely to be defensive or desperate because it's hard for young people to know what to say about boyfriends and girlfriends when things keep changing and the rules are unclear. There are some young people, I know, who claim that their relationships are entirely straightforward, and some who do enjoy perfectly happy relationships which occasionally last a lifetime. But in 30 years' work, I've never known any young people who haven't agonised along the way, who haven't secretly doubted themselves or privately wondered about the rightness of a particular relationship. At the age of thirteen – sixteen – nineteen there's so much to think about, so much to assimilate. Do I look okay? Am I funny? Will people like me this way? Would I be any good as a boyfriend or girlfriend? *Am* I any good? What do I feel, really? Am I normal? Is *this* normal?

In search of answers, young people frantically read problem pages; they watch television; they phone, they text, they talk to friends and – sometimes – they talk to professionals because they *do* get hurt and they *do* get stuck and they *do* find it hard to make sense of what they're experiencing. It's confusing. It's contradictory. Scientists might claim that whatever we choose to call 'love' is really just a biological need to attach, to propagate the species, to survive. Romantics might counter that 'true love' is something magical and mysterious, impossible to define. Young people wrestle with these perspectives, trying to interpret their own experience. How far should I trust my attraction to this person? Is it biological sex or magical love? What's the difference? Is it a mixture? What are my instincts telling me? Are they right or wrong? Should I trust them?

Yet the very idea of trusting our 'instincts' is tricky when instincts can sometimes be so right and at other times so wrong. The idea of anything being 'natural' is never as simple as it sounds and, whenever we're invited to consult our 'feelings', we're usually left none the wiser. So, young people carry on searching, searching for clarity, searching for answers, constantly positioning and re-positioning themselves on a continuum between different ways of understanding experience – the objective, observable and verifiable versus the subjective, intuitive and ineffable.

All this searching is important because whatever young people do or don't experience *and the sense they make of it* will inevitably affect their wise or unwise choice of partners in the future. This book is about helping young people make sense of their experience because, of course, the objective and the subjective are inseparable; our thoughts and feelings are always connected (Nussbaum 2001) and can't be compartmentalised neatly by young people or by counsellors. But at least we can talk together; we can wonder together; we can try to live with the uncertainty of not knowing (see Chapter 2).

Like most counsellors, I start from the assumption that the past affects the present; that family experiences affect the people we become and that loving and hating relationships are influenced by these things. Of course, things happen from time to time which feel magical and unpredictable but we usually end up feeling the way we do for reasons which make some kind of autobiographical sense.

It's a different kind of sense from the old notion of melancholic, sickly youths, shot through with Cupid's arrow, wandering aimlessly, pining for love or beaming ecstatically, madly in love and dancing all night under a smiling moon.

Romeo Montague is all of these things. For him, love is a jumble of contradictions:

> O heavy lightness! serious vanity!
> Mis-shapen chaos of well-seeming forms!
> Feather of lead, bright smoke, cold fire, sick health!
> Still-waking sleep, that is not what it is!
> This love feel I...

Romeo and Juliet, Act 1, Scene 1

I imagine Romeo coming to my counselling room, worried about Juliet and wondering what to do for the best, whereas Hamlet would be the disenchanted, cynical boy, intrigued by counselling but keeping his distance. It would take a lot for him to come and see me – I'd have to find some way of befriending him first – and then he'd only mention Ophelia in passing. We'd talk instead about his mum, his dad's death and about hating his step-dad.

I work in a school like any other school. At break times, there are young people pressed against each other, hugging and kissing. There are others joking and flirting with each other, and hundreds more sitting around simply enjoying each other's company. I work with them and with their teachers. Love is a preoccupation for us all. I listen to teachers who are arguing with partners at home and other teachers without partners, working flat out, only to be left exhausted at the weekend and wondering, 'What will become of me? Will I ever find someone for me? Will I ever have children?' I'm touched by their plight as I'm touched by the shy young person, longing for love, who sits in my counselling room and bravely tells me, 'I haven't got time for a boyfriend or girlfriend at the moment!'

Love is a preoccupation. But so is hate. For every two young people holding hands and gazing into each other's eyes at break time, there are two others who hate each other's guts and are busy organising rival armies. There are young people who come to see me, worried that someone is threatening to beat them up, that they're losing their friends or that a particular friend is refusing to talk to them. At break time, the bystanders and gossip-mongers are aware of the latest romances unfolding in different parts of the school, but they're also aware of the fights and feuds going on. There are hushed conversations in corridors, toilets and classrooms; some young people in tears, some offering advice, some hell-bent on revenge. These are the daily undercurrents of school life, not always visible but always there. Indeed, these are undercurrents wherever young people happen to be – at home, at work, in hospital, in prison – because love and hate are central parts of any young person's experience. Jenny can't decide whether to love or to hate the idea of a father out there somewhere, out of reach since she was two years old. For her, it's tempting to believe that he's a wonderful father, misunderstood and forever missing his long-lost daughter. But Jenny is also wise enough to know that he might be a heartless bastard who's never once thought of getting in touch with her.

Supporting young people as they learn to bear these feelings is difficult. Whether we work as counsellors, teachers, youth workers, social workers or in some other professional capacity, it's easier to enjoy young people when they're straightforwardly in love, when they're holding hands and gazing into each other's eyes. It makes them mellow and brings a smile to our faces. It's harder to know how to respond when they're gripped by an experience just as intoxicating – the experience of being *in hate*. The two are intimately connected, as the young man with L-O-V-E and H-A-T-E tattooed across his knuckles probably senses and as recent neurological research indicates (Zeki and Romaya 2008*). The most famous love story in Western literature is about hate as well as love. Romeo observes, 'Here's much to do with hate, but more with love…' (Act 1, Scene 1), while Juliet describes her boyfriend as 'My only love sprung from my only hate…' (Act 1, Scene 5).

In counselling, Jenny struggles to hold on to the possibility that her father might be a mixture of loveable and hateful qualities. But for other young people, this struggle is too much to bear: they split the world into one thing or the other, convincing themselves that other people are either to be adored or despised.

So we encounter some young people who seem to hate everybody and everything and, understandably, we avoid them. They're intimidating. We defend ourselves against them by complaining that they don't care, that they only think about themselves, that they don't appreciate the value of anything, that they're so *rude*…

The hatred these young people feel is often expressed in unacceptable, even criminal ways, but I think that hatred itself is normal in human beings. The third chapter of this book describes the inevitability of young people's hatred, its many expressions and meanings because, unless we understand and engage with hatred, we leave young people afraid of their capacity to hate and quite unable to regulate its expression. In other words, the more we avoid and refuse to think about it, the more hatred grows.

Our most famous love story is about hatred as well as love and it's about parents. Romeo and Juliet try to remain loyal to their parents but become more and more infuriated by them. Chapter 4 is about young people learning to bear mixed feelings about their parents and looking to make up for the times in their lives when they've really hated them. It describes ways in which boyfriends, girlfriends and people like counsellors find themselves caught up in these unconscious but crucial reparative processes.

The final chapter is about relationships breaking up; about young people ending counselling relationships and, by extension, ending relationships with boyfriends, girlfriends and other important people in their lives. Jenny's eight-month-long relationship with her boyfriend has almost certainly ended. But to mourn its loss and to move on, she and I will need to go back to the beginning, to Jenny meeting him for the first time and fancying him. And this is where I'll begin the book, with young people in and out of love, learning about love, because by the time they walk into my counselling room their feelings about love are never straightforward...

*Zeki and Romaya's research shows that, although love and hate are traditionally thought of as opposites, the same parts of the brain (the putamen and the insula) are activated in loving as in hating.

2

Young People in Love

There are some familiar stories… Leanne is going out with Joff and last week he cheated on her at a party. 'He was drunk, though,' she adds, 'and he told me he doesn't fancy that other girl anyway.'

A few weeks later, she's heard a rumour that Joff wants to finish with her and she's worried, not knowing what to think. 'He's not answering his phone and I've been round to his house but his mum says he's staying at his dad's.'

I ask what it would be like to split up with Joff, but Leanne won't contemplate that possibility.

When I see her next, the rumour has been sorted out, but they've had a row. Joff has accused *her* of cheating on *him*. 'All I did was talk to some of his mates!' she says. 'God, if I can't do that!'

'Then?'

'Then I don't know! Anyway, it's all right now,' she beams, 'because we talked last night and he admits he only gets jealous because he doesn't want to lose me.'

Two weeks later, she sits down and starts crying. They were both drunk and Joff wouldn't walk her home because he wanted to go to his friend's house instead. 'So I told him he had to choose between me and his friends and he said that if that's how it's going to be, then we might as well end it. So I said fine!' She sobs, wiping her eyes on her sleeve. 'God, I've been so stupid! I've made us break up and he means so much to me!'

'How much?'

'Everything! He means everything to me! I've never been out with anyone for as long as this!'

Suddenly she stops crying, reaches into her bag, pulls out her phone and checks for messages. Disappointed, she drops the phone back and starts crying again.

'You keep getting hurt, Leanne.'

'I love him so much!' she says, ignoring my comment. 'You know when you can't stop thinking about someone? Well, I can't stop thinking about him!'

I ask if that's love.

'It must be,' she says. 'I've never felt like this about anyone before…'

The next time we meet, she can barely contain herself, wide-eyed with excitement, showing me the ring that Joff has bought her. 'Guess what? He proposed and I accepted! Can you believe it? Our families don't know yet because I'm not old enough, but as soon as I'm sixteen we're going to tell them. Oh my God, I can't wait for my sixteenth birthday!'

I feel as if I'm sitting with Juliet in the Capulet family tomb and, even though I know what happens, I mustn't dampen her enthusiasm because she's never seen the play. I say I'm pleased she's happy but that things don't always go smoothly.

'I know,' she says confidently. 'But we've agreed that if one of us ever has a problem, we'll always discuss it together.'

Oddly, she barely mentions Joff at our next two meetings. When I ask about him, she says that everything's fine and she wants to talk about other things.

Finally, she mentions that the relationship has ended. 'It just didn't work out,' she says matter-of-factly, like a woman who has seen all of life. 'We both want different things at this stage in our lives. But we've agreed to stay friends.'

I say I'm sorry.

'No, it's fine,' she says. 'I've moved on. There's this really nice guy at the place where I work. But I'm going to see how it goes. I'm not going to rush into anything…'

LOVE AND PRACTISING

Leanne's story is familiar because it's a story about practising. Winnicott (1971) describes the play between a mother and her child as the way in which a child learns about itself and about other people by testing, trying things out with another person. In the same way, young people are constantly playing or – more accurately – *practising* for adult life with each other. Children practise monogamous relationships with a single best friend. They spend time in threesomes, seeing whether it's possible to be best friends with more than one person at the same time. Sometimes they see what it's like to have no friends at all, and sometimes they dare to make friends with whoever happens to be around.

Thirteen-, fourteen-, fifteen- and sixteen-year-olds take all that learning and push it a stage further into boyfriend and girlfriend relationships. As they separate from their parents, finding an alternative source of love becomes a preoccupation – finding it, trusting it, keeping it, ending it. There are young people who never actually meet their first boyfriend or girlfriend, because that relationship is conducted through the internet with someone on the other side of the world. But having practised speaking to that person every day via a keyboard, having practised sharing secrets and declaring love, it becomes possible to end the relationship and start with someone closer to home. In the school canteen at lunchtime, two young people meet for the first time. They start talking. They stay behind after school to talk when no one else is around. Eventually, they hold hands, they kiss, they start going round together and the process continues – practising, practising, practising. Like Romeo practising with his first girlfriend Rosaline, Leanne's frantic relationship with Joff allows her to practise a whole range of experiences in a very short period of time. She does this frantically because, like most young people, she's preoccupied with 'I love you'. What exactly do these words mean? What should I expect from love? What should it feel like? How can I trust another person's words? What proof of love should there be?

LOVE AND PROOF

Young people are forever asked, 'What are you feeling? Why did you do that?' They say they don't know because they don't, because it's usually the truth, however frustrating that may be for adults. But they hate not knowing. It's unsettling and it makes them anxious. What *am* I feeling? Why *did* I do that? The world rewards people for knowing; and when young people don't, they clutch at answers.

Alice is perplexed. For weeks she's been wondering whether or not to finish with Ricky, complaining that she doesn't know what she feels about him and that, in any case, he doesn't seem interested in her. 'If he was bothered,' she says, 'if he really cared about me, he'd show it.'

But today she's excited. 'You'll never guess!' she announces proudly. 'He's only gone and got a massive tattoo done on his arm! A tattoo of his name and my name! Together!'

It's hard for young people to be sure whether or not they really love each other. They worry, feeling that they *ought* to know. Alice and Ricky attempt to prove the authenticity and permanence of their love because now the whole world can see that they love each other '4 EVA'. Other young people hide the same underlying anxiety about not knowing with passionate reassurances ('I really do love you, honest!'), with expensive presents ('To show how much I love you!'), with engagement rings ('Because I'll always love you!') or with the sharing of secrets ('You're the only one I've ever told!'). Sometimes they hide their anxiety about not knowing with sex ('This *proves* how much I love you!')

'I really liked him!' Naomi says, dabbing her eyes. 'But now he doesn't want to go out with me any more and I know it's because he's been seeing *her*!'

She tells me that they had sex the first time they met. 'I wasn't that bothered to be honest, but he really wanted to do it and I was a bit drunk and I fancied him!'

'And then?'

'Then nothing! The next day he just said he didn't fancy me.' She shrugs her shoulders. 'Maybe it was for the best. I don't know.'

Naomi's may have been the latest in a long line of disingenuous boyfriends persuading girls that 'If you really love me, you'll have sex with me!' For young people, sex is partly about practising to be good at sex and partly – for boys – about enjoying as many orgasms as possible. But, for many young people, sex is also an implicit test of compatibility and commitment, 'Is he the right one? Does she really love me? Are we suited?' Sex becomes a way of anxiously *proving* love when the alternative is to wait and see, to live with not knowing. Because so many young people grow up with pervading uncertainty in their lives, they long to attach to someone reliable. They'll do anything to avoid the continuing anxiety of not knowing whether or not they're loved, whether or not they really matter. So for some, sex – with its promise of an orgasmic, if temporary, release from anxiety – appears to solve the problem. It never does, of course, as Naomi learns to her cost.

Not knowing is made harder by the rhetoric passed down by generations of love-sick poets. When it's 'true' love, they seem to say, *you'll know*! It'll hit you with a blinding flash. Your eyes will meet across a crowded room and – just like Romeo and Juliet – you'll *know*! Magazines trade on young people's search for some kind of proof. 'Does she really love you?' asks the problem page. 'Is he Mr Right?' asks the quiz. Even Juliet herself, on behalf of a million nervous young lovers, looks down from her balcony and wonders whether Romeo really means it:

> Dost thou love me? I know thou wilt say 'Ay,'
> And I will take thy word: yet, if thou swear'st,
> Thou mayst prove false...

> *Romeo and Juliet, Act 2, Scene 2*

Naomi allows herself to be rushed into sex as a test of true love and her boyfriend fails the test. There are other young people who try to bind their boyfriends and girlfriends to them with rules and expectations designed to remove any doubt from the relationship. To prove that they only have eyes for one person, they stop seeing all their friends. Or they take on fixed roles in the relationship – he the talker, she the listener; he the baby, she the parent; he speaking from the head, she from the heart. Because these roles are co-dependent – one can't exist without the other – neither person can function by themselves and so a mutual reliance is established. For the time being.

Without telling him, Ashley's girlfriend has gone and booked a holiday for herself and a couple of her friends.

'We've been going out together for over a year and she didn't say anything to me about it,' says Ashley. 'And normally we discuss everything. I thought I could rely on her but she's done this behind my back.'

I ask what she *has* said to him.

'She said she's sorry but she didn't realise it was such a big deal.'

'Is it?'

'Of course it is! It means we won't be able to see each other for the whole of the Easter holidays and the day she gets back from her holiday is the day before school starts, so that's no use! I just wish she'd consulted me.'

'Consulted you?'

'Yeah, if we're supposed to be going out, we should be consulting each other about everything.' He shakes his head in disbelief. 'I can't trust her if she's going to do stuff like this.'

'That sounds serious, Ashley.'

'It *is* serious! I mean, I really love her and everything but I feel betrayed.'

'Because she's done something without consulting you?'

He thinks for a moment. 'Does that sound stupid?'

I say it depends on the relationship and on how much freedom he and his girlfriend have to lead their own lives. 'It depends whether she didn't tell you because she didn't think it mattered or because she wanted to make a decision for herself and knew you'd be cross. I suppose it's about whether you can love each other but still have the freedom to decide things for yourselves. Does loving someone mean consulting them about everything? What happens if a relationship starts to feel a bit claustrophobic?'

He asks, 'Do you think that's what she thinks?'

I say I have no idea but that these questions are important.

He nods but looks confused, struggling to understand his girlfriend as more than just an extension of himself and angry with me for suggesting that the rules of love may not be quite as straightforward as he'd imagined.

LOVE AND PROMISES

For young people like Ashley, Naomi and Alice, the proof of love can also seem to lie in promises. Promises are so tantalising, so seductive ('I mean it! I promise! I really *do* love you!'). Young people can't help themselves: despite all their experience, all their disappointments, they still long to trust the promises people make, especially the promises of love. Perhaps *this* will be the promise that's kept? Perhaps *this* will be the dream that comes true? I suspect that marriage remains attractive, not only for Romeo and Juliet but for so many young people, because, despite everything, marriage represents a promise that can never be broken. And what could be better than that?

I think promises are so seductive because, from the very beginning of our lives, even as we lie curled up in a balmy womb, blissfully merged with our mothers in what Balindt (1968) calls a 'harmonious interpenetrating mix-up', it's as if a promise is implicitly made to us, a promise that this is what life will be like: we'll be loved and kept safe in the world. We're born and our parents are quick to make this promise explicit, 'I'll always be there for you!' they say. 'I'll always love you! I'll do anything for you!' We grow up, our confidence based on these and other promises. But, for many sons and daughters, these promises are quickly broken – broken cruelly and broken repeatedly. Fathers leave home without warning. New partners appear and disappear. Pregnancies are announced.

Young people hate it and are hurt by it whenever a promise is broken. There are the little, everyday promises – parents promising to be home from work at a certain time, promising to help with homework – and there are the bigger ones, the sweeping statements – parents promising always to 'be there', promising always to stay together, promising that nothing will change.

When so many promises have been broken, trusting other people becomes harder and yet *still* young people are seduced, looking to boyfriends and girlfriends to keep promises that their parents have never been able to keep. 'I won't be like the others,' says the boy with the handsome smile. 'I'll never hurt you,' says the girl with the kind eyes. 'I'll always be there for you,' says the shy, unassuming boy. 'I'll always love you,' says the girl in the tight, black dress.

I have to be very careful about the promises I make as a counsellor. I'm not a parent to the young people coming to see me but I'm parent-*like*. A similar set of hopes and longings are evoked. Perhaps this counsellor will understand me and like me? Perhaps he'll want to see me again? Perhaps he'll realise that I'm a good person really? Perhaps he'll think I'm special?

I do promise that there's hope and that counselling can be helpful. I *don't* promise to make things better; yet I suspect that all young people, beginning to invest in a relationship with me, secretly hope that I will, indeed, be able to make things better. The school they attend is usually making them all kinds of blithe promises. 'You'll get the very best education here,' say the teachers. 'We won't allow any bullying. We'll always respect and listen to your views, and if you work hard you'll succeed.'

I remember interviewing an entire cohort of three hundred young people in groups about their recent experience of school. They were in their last year of compulsory education and group after group was bitter about two things in particular. 'Nothing's happened about the Common Room!' they kept saying. 'Last year we were promised a Common Room and still nothing's happened! That's so *typical* of this school!' They also complained vehemently about the turnover of teachers in particular subjects and told me about one teacher in particular. 'Because he knew we'd already had so many teachers, he actually signed a piece of paper in front of us, promising that he wouldn't leave, and we had to sign something to say we'd work hard in his lessons. And then, a few weeks later, he left and didn't even tell us!'

I could say little. I wondered whether these particular promises cut deeply because the promise of having a Common Room was like the promise of a home and the promise of having a reliable teacher was like the promise of a reliable parent. I guessed that many of the young people felt so strongly because they'd been reminded of earlier betrayals in their lives.

I encourage young people to be realistic about counselling, going slowly and avoiding rushing into things with someone they barely know. 'We've only just met,' I say sometimes. 'I suggest we keep meeting because it'll take time to work out how much we can trust each other.' In our early meetings, I'm tested in the same subtle ways that young people test new step-parents, teachers, boyfriends and girlfriends. I'm offered bits and pieces of a life to see how I'll react, how much I'll remember, how much I'll take at face value and how tenacious I'll be when the going gets tough ('Will you want to keep meeting with me when you know what I'm *really* like?').

Invariably, we end up talking about loss. Thirteen-year-old Ryan sits staring out of the window, barely able to speak. His father died when he was eight. His mother has a new partner and is pregnant. 'I don't know,' he mumbles, unable to answer my questions. 'I've got a really bad memory. I can't remember things.' Not only has he lost his father but he's also lost a certain kind of relationship with his mother. He's moved house, moved school, lost his position as the man of the family and lost any naivety he might once have had about sex and death. He's struggling to adapt to so many losses, so many implicit promises broken.

Hillman (1964) describes life as a perpetual experience of betrayal after the 'primal trust' of birth. Separating from a symbiotic relationship with its mother, a baby quickly learns that she's no longer always there, isn't always able to protect her baby and doesn't always live up to her word. We live with this internalised sense of betrayal, argues Hillman. Slowly, very slowly, we develop a capacity to forgive our parents and an eventual understanding that with trust always comes the possibility of betrayal.

Young people find this hard to accept. There are adults who blandly promise, 'You can tell me anything! You can trust me! I won't judge you!' and, amazingly, some young people go along with these latest promises despite all that's happened in their lives, perhaps hoping for a womb-like safety they can't consciously remember but sense may still be possible. We talk in counselling about the promises that boyfriends and girlfriends make and about the need to go slowly, living with the anxiety of never being entirely sure whether or not a particular promise will be kept. I think that the sheer ordinariness of counselling (see Chapter 4), the fact that magic doesn't happen and that I don't make everything all right is initially disappointing but ultimately, I suspect, reassuring because the implicit message is that this is what relationships are like: trust is slow; affection grows; love is hard to quantify.

This is important learning because, in their anxiety, young people are inclined to rush, immediately idealising new boyfriends and girlfriends while demonising the old ones. It's a basic tenet of psychoanalytic theory (Klein 1957) that a baby loves *and* hates, idealises *and* demonises its mother – loving her when she provides and hating her when she doesn't. Understandably, the newborn baby concludes that it must have two mothers – a good one who provided everything at the beginning and a bad one who has since arrived, withholding everything. The baby, child, young person, adult spends a lifetime coming to terms with the fact that these two different mothers are one and the same person and that its parents are, in fact, a mixture of good and bad like everything else in the world.

This process of splitting a parent into good and bad is re-enacted at the expense of boyfriends and girlfriends. A young person typically falls in love with a wondrous being ('She's amazing!') who, inevitably, turns out to be less than wondrous. Admiration quickly turns to scorn ('She's a bitch!') unless the young person can find a way of coming to terms with the fact that this once-wondrous boy or girl may well be flawed but remains loveable nonetheless. Like a parent.

'I don't know what's the matter with me,' says Joe. 'I've fancied her for ages and now, the moment we start going out, I seem to have gone off her. I don't know what to do. And I can't tell her because it's unfair as I spent nearly a year trying to get her to go out with me!'

I ask what's changed.

'I used to think she was really special – really different from the others, you know? Really nice!'

'And now?'

'Don't know, really. I'm bored. We don't seem to be interested in the same things.'

'Maybe you don't know each other very well?'

Joe agrees. 'We don't know each other *at all*!'

'Maybe it'll take time,' I suggest. 'Maybe you never knew what she was like because she was just this amazing fairy princess and now you have to get to know a real person. Maybe she'll be a mixture of things for you to love and not love?'

As a counsellor, I spend a lot of time helping young people with this, whether we're talking about their boyfriends and girlfriends or their parents. We're working towards an acceptance that people – including parents – are no longer amazing or bitches. They're a mixture.

Typically, the crunch comes when the lovers argue for the first time. Some couples never dare to argue for fear of destroying an illusion of idealised love but, for those who can argue, the argument represents a turning point. Will it be possible for us to argue and still love each other? Or will our argument prove that we don't really love each other? If I get angry, will it end up destroying our relationship? Or can we love each other without necessarily liking everything about each other?

Promises offer a simplified, idealised world which doesn't account for people making mistakes, being selfish or having mixed feelings about each other.

Jono knows all about people breaking promises. A succession of men have come into his life and gone away again, all expressing undying love for his mother and all promising to be the reliable father he's needed. We sit down for our fortnightly counselling session and I ask how his latest plan to give up smoking has been going.

'Badly,' he says. 'Especially as my girlfriend's pregnant!'

Boys are forever telling me that their girlfriends are pregnant or 'might be' pregnant, so I don't react.

But he's convinced. 'We found out last week. She did a test and then she went to the doctor and did another one.'

I remember him telling me months ago that his girlfriend was on the pill *and* they were using condoms.

'Pill didn't work,' he says, 'and the condom split.'

According to boys, all condoms split. It's a badge of honour, as if their jet-propelled penis bursts through every condom and continues for several miles before eventually coming to a halt. 'Condom split! Yeah, the bloody condom split!' I know condoms are capable of splitting but I think a lot of bad workmen blame their tools (so to speak). I suspect that the condoms slide off because they were put on badly or never put on in the first place. They don't usually split.

However, Jono's condom officially split and here we are – Jono aged fifteen and his girlfriend, also fifteen, pregnant.

'She's going to keep it,' he says, 'because I don't believe in abortions and neither does she.'

Still taken aback, I ask how he's feeling.

'Excited!' he says. 'And nervous! I mean, I'm only fifteen and I haven't even got a job. But the good thing is that we can both fit into her bedroom and her mum's going to help us with the baby.'

I'm reminded of teaching novels where ill-matched young couples battled it out in damp basements, learning to look after their new-born baby and wondering what on earth had happened to their dreams. The novels always ended tragically, partly because tragedy was a good way of keeping the attention of teenage readers and partly because the novels were effectively a form of contraceptive warning in the days when schools weren't allowed to do much sex education. Moral disapproval hung over the protagonists. They were doomed. But for the young people reading these novels, there was always something exciting and grown-up about the thought of having a baby with your boyfriend or girlfriend.

Jono isn't pretending to be grown-up but these are early days. The next time we meet he tells me that he and Jacey are going for their first scan and, without breaking his train of thought, tells me that they were out the other night playing Man Hunt and a boy jumped out from behind a tree to capture Jacey, knocked her over and she fell on her stomach. From his hiding place, Jono saw it happen and threatened to beat up the boy if Jacey or the baby were hurt.

It dawns on me that 'Man Hunt' is another name for Hide-and-Seek. He and his pregnant girlfriend were out with their friends playing Hide-and-Seek in the park. But I sense that this story is really about the possibility of Jacey losing the baby and I wonder whether a part of Jono unconsciously hopes that this will happen, despite his threats to beat up that thought.

I don't suggest this. But with doomed young lovers in mind, I do suggest that life must feel strange at the moment.

'Everyone says I must be wishing it hadn't happened,' he says, 'but, to be honest, I'm glad. It means that we'll be having our kids early and then, when everyone else is having theirs, me and Jace will be sitting in the pub laughing because ours will have grown up!'

I'm impressed by his optimism, but I'm sceptical. Every time we meet, I expect to hear that he and Jacey have changed their mind about keeping the baby or – more probably – that they've broken up and he hates her and never wants to see her again. Because that's how the story usually goes.

But every time we meet, he has new things to tell. Baby equipment is really expensive, especially brand-new. He can't wait to leave school. Their sex life is rubbish at the moment but he doesn't mind. Jacey's good at getting alcohol because shopkeepers see her bump and think she must be over eighteen. And he really *is* going to give up smoking before the baby's born.

He seems to look forward to our meetings, needing to talk about all these things and needing to feel supported, not probed endlessly for doubts and misgivings. And, as time passes, I'm embarrassed by my original scepticism because I'm learning that, despite what I think I know about young people and despite all that's happened in his life, Jono has no intention of breaking his promise to Jacey or their baby.

LOVE AND RUMOURS

One day he tells me that they haven't been getting on so well lately because another boy has been spreading rumours about Jacey.

'I know it's complete bollocks,' he says, 'because I asked her and she said it wasn't true and I believe her. But then there was a rumour going round about *me* – just because I walked a girl home! Jacey heard about it and thought I was planning to get off with her. So I explained that I *had* to walk the girl home because it was late and she didn't have any money for a taxi.'

Jono and his girlfriend are practising for adult roles they must play in a few months' time. Perhaps, unconsciously, they tried to prove their love for each other with sex and then, unconsciously, tried to prove their commitment to each other with pregnancy. Now their anxiety about the situation is expressed through the 'rumours' Jono describes.

Eleven- and twelve-year-olds discuss rumours about friends – who's supposed to have said what about whom. Older young people are beset by rumours of more serious infidelities – things going on behind people's backs, people fancying other people, people having sex with people they shouldn't… Rumours are the cause of anger and tears, of late-night phone calls and, sometimes, of break-ups. But, in my experience, they're usually expressions of young people's *internal* doubts and fantasies about their boyfriends and girl-friends. Of course, there are some young people who start rumours and certainly pass on rumours because of jealousy or spite, but more often a simple miscommunication or in-nuendo is allowed to become a full-blown rumour because it expresses an unconscious doubt or fantasy *that already existed.*

Young people are effectively re-enacting the marital and extra-marital scandals described every day in newspapers and on television. Their own scandals of duplicity and un-faithfulness are discussed in playgrounds and corridors, in the hushed privacy of toilets or the leisurely surroundings of bedrooms – who allegedly said what about whom and who allegedly did what with whom. Elias and Scotson (1994) write about the 'gossip mills' of a community where the more threatened and insecure people are feeling, the more likely it is that gossip will be mistaken for fact. This is true of rumours. Rumours are likely to be treated as facts depending on the level of collective anxiety that exists about whatever underlying issue the latest rumour addresses. The rumour that a girl has chlamydia quickly becomes a statement of fact because *everyone* is anxious about chlamydia. The rumour that one boy's girlfriend cheated on him becomes a fact because *everyone* is anxious about their girlfriend cheating on them. Collective anxieties are projected on to other people and called 'rumours'.

Alisha loves her boyfriend, but he might be going to split up with her, she says, because there are untrue rumours going round that she had sex with a boy on a school trip. I don't know Alisha's boyfriend but I'm quite sure that the reason why these 'rumours' affect him is because, inevitably, he wonders what Alisha gets up to when he's not around and whether she's as loyal to him as she insists.

I agree with her that these rumours are unfair and annoy-ing. 'I suppose everyone wonders what it would be like to be close to someone else,' I say. 'We might really love someone but still fancy other people a bit.'

She thinks about this.

'You and your boyfriend might love each other and have no plans to split up but, from time to time, you might both wonder what it would be like to go out with someone else.'

'Of course,' she says, 'but that doesn't mean I don't love him, does it!'

We pause, thinking about this before moving on to talk about something else. I hope that by acknowledging the underlying anxiety and making it seem normal, we've taken away some of its destructive power. The rumours may now feel less awful, and Alisha may be able to deal with them more confidently.

As I've said, she and her boyfriend devote so much time to rumours because rumours express anxieties. Do you really love me? How much do you love me? Do you love me as much as you love other people? How can I be sure that you love me? Why can't you *prove* that you love me? These questions beset young people because they're the questions we ask originally and most urgently of our parents.

LOVE AND PARENTS

Romeo and Juliet's problems are caused by their parents, and Hamlet's relationship with Ophelia is undermined because of his feelings about his parents. Parents are invisibly present whenever a young person is talking with me in counselling about a boyfriend or girlfriend.

For example, Scarlett's boyfriend is away at university. She visits him at weekends but feels that she's the one making all the running. She can't decide what to do. 'When we're together he can be really nice,' she says, 'but sometimes he doesn't seem to care whether I'm there or not. The other weekend I was staying with him and he and his flatmates were sitting round looking at porno magazines!'

In the school holidays, she flies off to visit her father in Italy. 'But he never comes here to see me or my brother,' she complains, 'and when I'm staying with him in Italy he's always out working or visiting friends.'

'Sounds a bit like your boyfriend, Scarlett.'

She thinks about this.

'It sounds like it's hard to give up on the people who are supposed to be there for you.'

She fights it, but slowly her eyes fill and, weeping, she starts to talk properly, for the first time, about her father – her earliest memories of him, the affair which took him away from the family, the anger and hurt she feels and why she's never been able to talk to him about this for fear of driving him further away.

Unlike Scarlett, Danny never mentions his parents if he can help it. But they're always implicitly part of our conversation as he talks about his girlfriend Roz, about meeting up with her at weekends, about their friends, their music, their clothes and all the zany things they do together which he enjoys recounting.

As soon as I ask about his mum and dad, he shuts up.

His parents are separated. His father drinks. His mother is pregnant by a new partner and this man has recently moved into the house. I know these things because I've asked and Danny has reluctantly answered my questions before returning quickly to talking about Roz and their friends. Then his mood lifts. It's as if he's saying, 'Things at home are horrible and I can't talk about them, but when I'm with Roz I'm happy because I don't have to think about my stupid parents.'

Weeks go by. He doesn't have to keep meeting with me but he does, continuing to talk about his friends, their loyalties and disloyalties, their relationships with each other and the ways in which those relationships keep changing. I no longer push him to talk about his parents because I think he's talking about them and trying to make sense of them all the time – obliquely – through talking about his friends, their likes and dislikes, jealousies and betrayals. I let him talk. He talks about loving Roz but feeling disappointed whenever she lets him down or hurts his feelings. Weeks later, he says he's worried that she might be going to dump him.

I want to say, 'Like your dad dumped your mum?' but I don't.

Bryony is different again from Danny and Scarlett in that she talks *constantly* about her parents. Bryony's in love with another girl, 'And they won't let me see her! I met up with her in town the other day and they found out and now I'm grounded for a month!'

We discuss the ins and outs of what's happened and how she feels. We explore practical possibilities, but Bryony insists that there's no room to manoeuvre.

'I can't talk to them. They don't listen to anything I say. I used to be able to talk to my sister, but even she seems to be on their side now! I used to be able to tell her things, but now she's got her boyfriend and she spends all her time with him so I don't bother trying to talk to her any more. And of course, my parents think her boyfriend's wonderful! My dad thinks the sun shines out of his arse!'

'And not out of yours...'

'You could say that!' she laughs. 'My dad would only be happy if I was at home all the time, doing schoolwork in my room.'

'Not fancying other girls!'

She laughs again.

'Maybe you're telling him something important,' I suggest. 'That you're not like your sister...'

'I'm not!'

'And maybe you're telling your sister something...'

'Like what?'

'Like feeling let down by her? Pissed off with her?'

'I *am* pissed off with her,' Bryony confirms. 'We used to be able to talk about things before she started going out with Mr Perfect!'

'And you miss that?'

She pauses and avoids my eye. 'Anyway,' she begins again, 'if they think I'm going to stop seeing my friends just because I'm grounded, then they've got another think coming! I'll climb out of my bedroom window and I don't care if they find out!'

In so many ways, boyfriends and girlfriends allow young people to speak to their parents and to speak *about* their parents. Romeo and Juliet make a statement to their feuding families by daring to be together. All sorts of things will probably be going on under the surface in Bryony's family. She has a sense of her sister as the favoured child, of losing a sister she could talk to and of losing a certain kind of relationship with her parents. There may well be feelings about lesbianism which are hard for the family even to talk about, and there will certainly be strong feelings about family rules as Bryony and her sister get older and demand more independence. I know nothing about Bryony's girlfriend, but in many families there are also feelings about ethnicity, culture and social class provoked by the introduction into the family of a boyfriend or girlfriend from a different background. All these things will be provoking discussions between Bryony's parents which may well be affecting their own relationship. So Bryony may love her girlfriend very much but her choice of girlfriend will also be a roundabout, unconscious way of getting the family to address some of these issues. Part of my job will be to help her think about what she's really trying to tell the family.

Vicki is also trying to tell her family something. She's under pressure to give up her boyfriend whose reputation as a bad lad is well known. 'Trouble is, I love him!' she says. 'I know he's done some bad things and been in trouble with the police. But if people took the time to get to know him, they'd realise that he's not really like that. He wants to change – I know he does! He says I'm the best thing that's ever happened to him. You should have seen him the other day – he was actually crying, telling me about how his dad used to treat him and his little brother. It pisses me off when people think they know what he's like.'

'And think they know what *you're* like?'

'Exactly!'

Vicki's choice of boyfriend attempts to tell her parents something important about herself. There are other girls who also choose difficult boyfriends – boys in trouble with the police, boys who drink too much, boys with troubled family histories – because they believe they can change the boy's behaviour, heal his hurt. They rarely succeed, but I often wonder how much they attempt unconsciously to heal a rift with their own fathers – a rift usually begun when they were twelve or thirteen, when they were beginning to stay out later, dress in more womanly ways and voice their own opinions. As a consequence and through no fault of their own, they suddenly lost the approval of their fathers.

Layla says that things with her boyfriend are good. 'We've been going out for two months and three days. In fact, we've just had our two-month anniversary and guess what? He bought me sixty-one red roses! That's a rose for every day that we've been going out.'

'He sounds nice, Layla.'

'He is! My dad doesn't like him, though, because he says we're spending too much time together and I should be spending more time with the family.'

'What do you say?'

'I say that I *do* spend time with the family, and if he got to know Sean he might actually like him.'

'What does your dad say?'

'He says that Sean's not good enough for me. But the trouble is that *nobody* would be good enough for my dad. He thinks all boys should like what he likes and agree with him about everything and, if they're lucky, he might let them talk to me one day. God, just because he's my dad, he thinks he *owns* me!'

I listen to lots of daughters talking about their fathers where the relationship has got stuck in exactly the same place. Typically, the daughter's story goes, 'When I was young, we were really close. But once I started secondary school it changed and now all he ever does is criticise me.'

Fifteen-year-old Shannon talks about how things with her father have changed. 'I used to be his favourite,' she says, 'and he used to call me his princess. But now we hardly speak.'

She's going out with Kyle who's twenty. They drive around in Kyle's car, sometimes picking up her friends who squeeze into the back seat while Shannon sits in the front, next to her boyfriend, her champion.

I know it can be hard for fathers to adjust to their daughters getting older but their poor daughters are usually mystified as to what they've done wrong. They thought they were doing the right thing – getting on with the difficult task of growing up, 'But now he says he hates my clothes and hates my friends and I'm a disappointment to him!'

Justine has sex with lots of boys and, as a result, gets called a slut by lots of boys which makes coming to school pretty unbearable.

I ask about life at home.

'It would actually *hurt* my dad to hug me,' she says.

I wonder what she's hoping to get from our relationship because, like any counsellor, teacher or other professional working closely with young people, I can be a father-figure or mother-figure. I can be demonised and I can be idealised. Without warning, I can be treated as if I'm a parent who doesn't understand or even care, while at other times I can be treated as if I'm the most wonderful parent who understands absolutely everything. More often than not, I'm cast as a benign parent-figure to whom young people look for approval.

Fourteen-year-old Freya's need for approval is entirely unspoken. Today, we're meeting in an empty classroom because our normal counselling room is being redecorated. She tells me that she hasn't seen her father for over a year, then tells me that she thinks she looks disgusting – her face, her body – everything, she says. Suddenly she gets up and goes to the other side of the room, climbs on to a desk and stands looking out of the window before turning, smiling and walking back unsteadily towards me across the tops of the desks, finally jumping down in front of me, embarrassed.

I smile and say nothing but feel like the father of a four-year-old daughter who calls, 'Look, Daddy! Look at me walking across these desks without falling!' while, at the same time, I feel like the father of a fourteen-year-old daughter showing me her body as she walks down a precarious, imaginary catwalk.

With Freya, it's enough to smile. It's all she needs. In our next session, she sits opposite me, gets out all her make-up and, very carefully, holding a little mirror, dabs on mascara and pale-blue eye shadow.

Most teenage daughters need the benign, supportive, non-sexual admiration of their fathers as they take their first steps into the world of men. Dressed up in their newest clothes, they can practise with a father ('How do I look, Dad?') knowing that he'll admire ('You look really glamorous!') *without doing anything.* But some daughters get a jealous, disapproving and implicitly sexualised response from their fathers ('You're not going out like that! You look like a tart!') which leaves them confused, ashamed and sad. They suffer the unfairness of brothers being allowed to stay out later and attend mixed sleepovers while they're made to stay at home for fear of someone other than their fathers claiming their affection before the big day comes and they're officially 'given away' at the altar.

Relationships with mothers are sometimes easier ('I can tell my mum everything! She's my best friend!') but charged in other ways. Emma tells me about kissing a boy last night but then getting beaten up by the boy's girlfriend and all her friends. 'He never told me he was going out with anyone!'

We agree about the unfairness of getting beaten up as if what happened was all her fault.

'Doesn't matter, though!' she laughs gaily. 'I don't care!'

Then she tells me about her mother having affairs with lots of men while still married to her father and about how you can't trust women.

Our work together will be about making sense of this statement because, until she can make sense of her mother, it'll be hard for Emma to make sense of herself. Why *do* people have affairs? Does it mean that my mum never really loved my dad? Was it my dad's fault that they split up? Did my mum and dad's feelings for each other change? Or was it *my* fault? Was it because I was difficult at home? Should I try to be perfect?

Emma starts missing a lot of school and we don't meet until three months later.

'I've been okay,' she says, sitting down. 'I was going out with a boy – or I thought I was until last night when he texted me to say he didn't want to see me again.' In fact, she's been going out with lots of boys during the last three months, she tells me, and having sex with all of them. 'If that's what they want to do then I let them because, to be honest, I can't be bothered any more. I'm never going to get anyone nice.'

'Because boys are only interested in one thing?'

'Yeah! And because of the way I look. I *hate* the way I look!' She's immaculately made up, with careful highlights in her hair, a slim body and pretty face. 'I hate myself,' she repeats. 'My friends say, 'Oh you're really nice looking, Emma', but I look at myself in the mirror and I think I look disgusting.'

It would be pointless to contradict her. I understand her to mean that she *feels* hateful and *feels* disgusting – getting used by boys for sex and never finding anyone who'll love her properly. Then I remember her mother. When Emma and I started meeting three months ago, she was refusing to speak to her mother, having left home after a row with her mother's boyfriend.

'I still haven't spoken to her,' says Emma, 'and I don't care! She tried to speak to me at Christmas but I wouldn't speak to her because, if she really cared, she'd never have chosen that man over me, the way she did. I'm never going to speak to her again.'

'Because it feels like she betrayed you?'

'Yeah!'

'And that hurts more than anything...'

She looks away.

'So you're not going to forgive her...'

'That's right!'

'And you might wish you could forgive her but you can't...'

Emma nods.

'Because your mother doesn't realise what she's done. And how much it hurts and how much you hate her for what she did. And how sometimes you hate yourself for not speaking to her but you can't change anything because she's the one who hurt *you*...'

She nods again.

I wonder to myself whether sex with boys has become Emma's way of re-enacting an experience of her mother who, in the middle of a row, seemed to choose her boyfriend over her daughter. Because now, no sooner does Emma get someone for herself – someone promising love, someone she allows inside her – than that person withdraws and she's left feeling worthless, exactly the way she felt after her mother appeared to side against her. And this experience is re-enacted with boys, day after day, as if Emma is hoping for a different outcome every time while proving to herself that the outcome will always be the same.

'So it feels as if nothing can change,' I repeat.

She agrees.

I say nothing. I wait. Until she feels that her anger and hurt have been properly acknowledged, nothing *can* change. All I've been doing is trying to offer her some of that acknowledgement.

'She'd have to get in touch with me,' Emma says. 'I'm not getting in touch with her – no way!'

I nod and say nothing. But there's movement here. She's no longer averse to being contacted by her mother and her mother *did* try to contact her at Christmas. Now, even if they can meet and argue with each other, that'll be progress. Things may get said. Emma may feel that her mother has heard and then the need to use sex endlessly to re-enact an experience of her mother may change.

The next time we meet, she tells me that she hasn't had sex with anyone recently. She talks about two boys. 'I don't know what to do. I really like Gavin because I can talk to him and I know he's a virgin so he's not interested in *that*. But I've known Eddie for ages and I've always fancied him a bit. He texted me the other day,' she giggles, 'and he's so cheeky. All he said was, "I really want to fuck you, Emma!"'

I resist the temptation to tell her which boy has my instant preference. Instead, we talk about these opposites because I think they represent opposite parts of Emma: emotional Gavin and physical Eddie, innocent and experienced, non-sexual and sexual. I think they also represent opposite ways of seeing her mother – as benevolent and benign or as hostile and selfish. The boy she chooses will effectively be an interpretation of her mother. But Emma and I will spend a lot of time before then discussing the possibility that her mother may be a mixture.

As the months have gone by, Emma's mother may well have been suffering as much as her daughter. I sometimes run workshops for parents anxious to find out whether their sons' and daughters' behaviour is normal. They worry about enforcing rules and usually react to their sons and daughters in terms of their own adolescent experience. After one particular workshop I remember arranging to meet with a mother who felt unable to continue living with her fifteen-year-old daughter.

She told me that the situation at home was impossible because her daughter was disobeying all the rules. 'For example, last week she stayed out and I discovered the next day that she'd been down at the playing fields all night with boys!' She looked at me angrily. 'I'm not having it! I'm not!'

I asked about her own adolescence.

Her own mother had been strict, she said. *Her* mother would never have tolerated this behaviour.

'And boys?'

'What about boys?'

'Did you have sex with boys when you were that age?'

She was staggered that I dared to ask. Her face reddened, her eyes filled with tears and she said that she'd once had sex with a boy – yes – and it had been the one-night stand which had produced her daughter.

Arguments at home about 'suitable friends' and 'being in by a certain time' always have sexual connotations. I've met with many parents determined to protect their sons and (especially) their daughters from the unsatisfactory early sexual experiences they suffered themselves. I've met with others, clearly jealous of their sons' and daughters' greater sexual opportunities and more relaxed, confident approach to sex.

Nina and I are meeting for the first time. She lives with her mother but they haven't been getting on recently because her mother disapproves of Nina's new boyfriend.

'Just because he's a few years older than me, my mum seems to think he's only interested in one thing. But I've told her that I'm not ready for that. I've talked to him about it and I know he's happy to wait.'

Before our session ends, she mentions that her mum also has a new boyfriend and that he's started staying over at weekends. 'I hate him,' she says with venom. 'I really hate him!'

I imagine that getting a boyfriend of her own has been Nina's way of dealing with her mother's sex life. She probably relishes her mother's anxiety about an underage relationship and probably longs for the argument where she can say, 'Well you do it, Mum, so why shouldn't I?' Our work together will involve thinking a lot about the circumstances of her parents' split, about her relationship with her father, about the things she misses and wishes about him and about the fact that a man other than her father is now sleeping in her mother's bed.

'It must have been weird when he started staying over, Nina.'

'It was! I hate it!'

'Because he isn't your dad?'

'He's nothing *like* my dad!' she says. 'I hate him! I don't even want to think about it!'

And we pause, thinking about it together.

Most young people try to rationalise away their parents' sex lives ('It's their life! It's up to them what they do!') because they find the idea disturbing. Some report overhearing their parents in the next bedroom at night.

'I keep my music on,' says Artan, 'otherwise I can hear them!'

Taylor tells me, 'I saw my dad going into the bathroom this morning with a condom dangling from his dick!'

Boys are particularly disturbed by the sexuality of their mothers but won't talk about it, swinging between 'I hate my mum!' and 'If anyone does anything to my mum, I'll kill them!' They'll talk about what life was like when their parents were still together and, like Hamlet, they'll talk about hating their step-dads. But talking about all those Freudian feelings is too much. Again like Hamlet, they're scornful and protective of their mothers in equal measure, needing their mothers' support but embarrassed by it and sometimes treating their girlfriends as they treat their mothers. Like mothers, girlfriends are supposed to understand intuitively without needing an explanation; they're supposed to love unconditionally, regardless of their boyfriend's impossible behaviour; they're supposed to forgive his every childish, selfish act.

'Look, I'm not your mother, okay!'

'What are you on about? I'm not expecting you to be!'

We carry internalised relationships with doting or difficult parents around in our heads and these relationships are re-enacted to a greater or lesser extent with boyfriends and girlfriends. Bramley (2008) argues that the relationships we make with partners in later life are unconsciously influenced by our earliest relationships with our mothers and – probably – our fathers. 'In adulthood, partner choice always contains in some form the search for the blissful aspects of early infancy. At the same time, there is hope that the new union will make up for all that disappointed in the old' (p.15). I often listen to young people complaining, ostensibly about a boyfriend or girlfriend but, at another level, always about their parents, 'I don't like the way she's always trying to control me... I hate the way he talks to other girls... I always listen to him but he never listens to me... It feels like I'm trapped... I can't tell her what I really feel in case she starts crying... She embarrasses me in front of my friends!' A parallel conversation about parents is evoked equally powerfully whenever young people talk admiringly about their boyfriends or girlfriends, 'She just seems to know what I'm feeling... He totally trusts me... I can tell her anything and she's never fazed... I know he's always going to take my side, whatever I do!'

Relationships with boyfriends and girlfriends can certainly re-enact existing relationships with parents but, more interestingly, they also become opportunities to re-interpret and amend those relationships. Some young people effectively tell me that, 'With this boy, I don't have to fight the way I've always fought with my dad!' or 'With this girl, I can say sorry in ways I've never been able to say sorry to my mum!' They often report that relationships at home have improved since they started going out with a particular boyfriend or girlfriend, as if something is easier now, as if a weight has been lifted.

A boyfriend or girlfriend's own parents are – themselves – sometimes part of the attraction, providing a fresh start and further opportunity to practise doing things differently. Fourteen-year-old Sachin, for example, is staying at his girlfriend's house because of the rows at home with his own parents. 'I get on really well with her family,' he enthuses. 'Her mum says I can stay as long as I want because I'm practically a member of the family anyway! When I'm there I help out with everything – the cleaning, the washing-up, the cooking – and I never do that at home. Last weekend me and her dad cleared out the shed together.'

Because of his age, Sachin isn't allowed to go off and live with someone else's parents, even if his own don't mind. Legally, it's not that simple. He'll almost certainly have to go back home. But he's already told his own parents that his girlfriend's are better in every possible way. 'I'd do anything for her mum and dad,' he tells me. 'If I didn't have them, I don't know what I'd do!'

'Because they enjoy having you around…'

'Yeah.'

'And you can be loving and helpful with them…'

'Definitely!'

'But at home you're too angry about all the things that have happened?'

For many young people, this comparison with another person's parents is vital, shedding a favourable or unfavourable light on their own. Boyfriends and girlfriends unwittingly become part of a re-evaluation and sometimes a creative reworking of original relationships at home which have become stuck. With a loyal boyfriend or girlfriend, sons and daughters are now less isolated in the family. Now there are opportunities to offer that boyfriend or girlfriend the love and concern that's impossible to express at home and, in so doing, young people are able to prove to themselves that they're not the bad children they always worried about becoming (see Chapter 4). So choosing a particular boyfriend or girlfriend can be an implicit attack on parents and all that they represent, but it can also be a peace offering, a way of saying to them, 'I'm sorry I behaved so badly, hating you so much. Look! I've brought home the person I love to share with you.' Young people report things like, 'She gets on really well with my mum – the two of them are always talking!' or 'My parents have said he can come on holiday with us.' It's as if the parents have been presented with an unsolicited gift. Now there are opportunities for sons and daughters to be affectionate and kind, polite and considerate in front of their parents. Sometimes there are opportunities to ask parents about their own early relationships, even their mistakes, as young people grow more confident and better able to talk

about all sorts of things, including the great unmentionable
– sex.

LOVE AND SEX

Mossy talks dismissively about girls because talking fondly
about them would be embarrassing. 'Treat them mean and
keep them keen – that's what my dad reckons! You can't let a
woman get close or she'll get attached,' he tells me, a sprinkle
of stubble around his fifteen-year-old smirk. 'I reckon it's
better to screw them and move on!'

He's started this macho banter recently. I don't know
whether I'm being tested to see whether I'll offer some predictable homily about the importance of men respecting
women or whether Mossy (whom I've known since he was
eleven) is merely strutting his adolescent stuff and letting me
know that he's not eleven any more. I know he's (secretly) as
vulnerable as any boy and, in a crisis, would be perfectly kind
and loyal to a girlfriend, provided that none of his mates were
watching. So, in that sense, I'm not worried about his sexism.
I'm not going to collude with it, but nor am I going to mock
it. I suspect that the issue behind this banter is *our* relationship, *our* fondness for each other and whether we can find a
way of honouring our feelings without getting embarrassed.

'I suppose liking other people can be embarrassing,
Mossy.'

'What d'you mean?'

'I mean, it can be embarrassing liking friends and liking
people at school.'

'Depends on what you mean by liking!' he says. 'I like my
friends but I wouldn't want to have sex with them!'

'Exactly!' I say. 'That's the problem, isn't it? Everyone's
worrying about sex all the time and that makes it hard just
being friends with people.'

'Maybe,' he concedes, 'but I still don't really get what you're on about.'

'Well, for example, you and I are friends,' I say. 'We like each other and we trust each other quite a bit. But other people might think that was strange.'

'That's their problem, then!' he says. 'Fuck them, if that's what they think!'

I agree with him and am happy to change the subject because we've just agreed implicitly that we like and trust each other. That's enough. That's a lot. Boys don't go up to their male friends and say 'I like you!' Instead, they grunt and punch their friend on the shoulder – quite hard. It means 'I like you!' but the affection has to be translated into a macho behaviour to allay their homophobic anxiety. For young people like Mossy, talking about sex usually involves talking about much more than sex.

It's the same with Sophie. She tells me about sex with her boyfriend. 'Whenever we're together, it's all he wants to do! It's like he's obsessed with sex or something! And if I don't want to do it, he goes into a really bad mood until I let him.'

I ask if she tells him what she *does* want to do.

'I do tell him,' she says, 'but it doesn't make any difference. He just keeps going on and on until I give in.'

I ask what kind of sexual relationship she'd like to have.

'I don't know,' she says. 'I *like* sex, don't get me wrong. But I don't want to do it all the time and sometimes, like when I'm on my period or when I'm really tired, I don't want to do it at all – no way!'

'And he doesn't understand that?'

'Doesn't seem to,' she says, 'or he can't be bothered to understand!'

There's a wider issue. Her mother slips in and out of hospital, in and out of depression, and, from what I gather, Sophie does all the cooking and cleaning in the evenings while her father and elder brothers sit around watching television. Her future as a servant of men seems assured despite coming to school every day and planning to do a childcare course at college.

My problem is that simply *telling* her to be more assertive will make no difference. She'll share my indignation, but our fulminations won't affect her ability to manage the situation the next time her boyfriend wants his way. With Sophie, it's deeper than that. It's about what she's worth, about her fear of having no boyfriend to go around with in a world where she's always felt alone. So far, she's survived all that life has thrown at her, and she'll survive this boyfriend, I'm sure, give or take the odd pregnancy scare, the odd infection. What matters more is her confidence to make choices and her sense of deserving more than just a quick one before the second half of the match begins.

I ask about her ideal man.

She jokes about famous film stars but then, without hesitation, describes him. 'He'd be really nice to me. He'd be quite good looking, but I wouldn't mind if he was ugly because looks don't really matter. He'd have a decent job and we'd go out together quite often. And, if we had kids, he'd really care about them.'

'And sex?'

'What do you mean?'

'Well, what would your sex life be like?'

'Don't know really. We'd *have* sex because all couples have sex but it would be more… I don't know!'

'Relaxed?'

'Yeah. Not so serious! Not doing it all the time.'

'More what *you* want?'

'Yeah!'

'Because you matter…'

'Do I?'

Her question stops me in my tracks. Conventional counselling theory dictates that we develop a sense of mattering from good early experiences in our lives (Gerhardt 2004) and that counselling reconnects us with these, helping us recognise that we've been loved and are still loveable. But Sophie has very little of this early experience to draw on. She knows how to survive with a shrug and a smile but with little sense of really mattering. Boyfriends get away with it because, deep down, she believes the scathing things they say about her.

Her question hangs in the room... *Do I matter?*

I want to say yes, but worry that this is to make myself feel better because I'm touched by her lack of confidence. Would she ever be able to believe and internalise such an assertion?

I decide to take the plunge. 'You do matter,' I say, 'enormously. You're kind and funny and honest and good at things. You're loyal to your friends. You're determined.'

'Really?'

A parent might say these things. If she can consider that they might possibly be true and that our meetings continue because she *does* matter, then some long-lost sense of worth, hidden in the dust of other people's disdain, might get a spring clean. And if this can happen, then she might just discover what it's like to feel more confident. Confident enough to say no.

Michael's problem isn't saying no. Quite the opposite. He roams the streets, attaching himself to any boys who'll let him go around with them and won't beat him up. Because that's what usually happens. 'Everyone beats me up,' he says. 'They think it's funny because I'm small.'

He's also spotty and scruffy and always in trouble with the police but, for a while, fourteen-year-old Michael was going out with a girl, loving her until he discovered that his twelve-year-old friend had asked her for a blowjob, 'And she gave him one.'

Today he tells me that he has some good news and some bad. 'Good news is I'm going out with a girl called Angel!'

I say I'm pleased for him.

Apparently, they met in the pub where she's living with her uncle. 'She's about a year older than me but I prefer older women,' he says with an absolutely straight face. 'Well, *girls*...'

'And the bad news?'

'Bad news is that we've had unprotected sex four times.'

In the school where I work as the counsellor, I also teach a lot of sex education which means that I'm a reliable source of free condoms. The more confident students come on their own to get supplies. The less confident ones come with a friend and the very unconfident students – always boys – come in large groups, leaning against the walls of the corridor outside my room and dodging each other's insults as they wait their turn to say, 'Yeah, me too. I need some!'

I give each boy a supply, knowing that the vast majority of these condoms will be used for the boys' own, solitary purposes.

Having waited at the back of the pack, the last to ask for condoms is always the smallest boy, shuffling forward, resentful, obliged to go through all this in order to save face. 'Yeah, me too!' he says, avoiding my eye.

I give him a supply. He pushes the condoms deep into his rucksack and hurries off without saying goodbye.

The sex education I do is very factual. In an ideal world, I'd have time to get to know each class and we'd be able to talk honestly about our hopes and fears and feelings. But there isn't an exam in sex education and so the subject gets squeezed to the edges of the curriculum and, in some schools, squeezed out altogether. In the brief time I have with each class, I talk a bit about the importance of relationships and love, but the young people sitting there are far more interested in hard information about sex than in my platitudes because, without that information, they're vulnerable. Like Romeo and his friends, they joke and tease each other about sex because they're *anxious* about sex. The more they know, the more confident and relaxed they feel and the less inclined they are to take their anxieties out on other people. So although reducing unplanned pregnancies and sexually transmitted infections are important governmental aims, I think that the more important reason for providing good, factual sex education is to reduce anxieties about sex which cause so much unhappiness. Without information, young people mock the ignorance of others to hide their own ignorance; they project their own anxieties about sexual experience and performance on to others and attack it. Most bullying has a sexual dimension.

Sitting there, waiting for me to begin, they don't laugh and they don't snigger. For me to suggest that they don't already know everything there is to know about sex would be a mistake, so I begin by saying that I'm quite sure they know most of this stuff already but that there may be the odd bit of information that's new and that it'll therefore be worth listening. Reassured, they listen, not because I'm a famous disciplinarian or a particular authority on sex but because they're desperate to pick up anything they don't already know. Sometimes they ask questions but more often they're too embarrassed to ask and it's my job to anticipate the questions they *would* ask if only it wasn't so embarrassing. I'm frank, which surprises them but is also, evidently, a relief. 'Does the foreskin have to be pulled back before sex? Do girls pee out of their vaginas? Does sex hurt? What if the penis is too small? In anal sex, what happens to the shit? How do you know if someone wants to have sex? What's the point of ribbed condoms?'

LOVE AND SEXUALITY

In passing, we talk about gay sex ('What do gay people actually do in bed?') and, at this point, they can't help it – they snigger. Amongst groups of boys, someone will always say to a particular boy, 'Hey, this is the bit about you, Neil! You'd better listen to this!' Neil tells them all to shut up and assures them that he's not gay. But once we've talked about gay sex and said the previously unsayable, the boys seem to relax, their anxiety lessened.

This is important because, amongst boys, homophobic anxiety is everywhere. I remember working with one particular group of boys for six weeks. This hadn't been set up as a sex education group although we'd talked about sex from time to time. Instead, it had been a group designed to give the boys a chance to talk about all sorts of things, including each other.

It was our last session. We sat in a rough circle, drinking hot chocolate and waiting to begin.

In an adjoining room, a boy their age was meeting with an older boy who was acting as his academic mentor. As I was explaining this to the group, the door of the adjoining room opened and the two boys left together.

'Are they gay?' asked Joel.

I said I didn't know and it wouldn't matter.

A couple of boys muttered to each other about 'benders'.

'I'll go and look!' announced Joel, getting up and disappearing into the adjoining room.

We waited for him to come back.

'I knew it!' he called from inside the room. 'They've been *doing it*!' And he re-appeared with a condom hanging from his fingers.

We laughed, knowing that he'd taken the condom from his wallet in order to make the joke.

Our session began, but comments about people being gay or not gay continued. My guess was that the boys were more anxious than usual because they'd shared some important things in this group and now it was our last session. It was ending and they couldn't decide whether to honour or deride their intimacy, hence the running commentary about people being gay or not gay.

Our last exercise involved an empty chair being added to the circle. Whoever had the empty chair on his right could invite another member of the group to come and sit next to him for a reason, and I gave examples of the kinds of reasons the boys might want to think about... 'Because I've got to know you better in this group... Because you're a mate... Because we support the same team... Because what you said about your mum is true about my mum as well...' If the invited person was happy with the reason then he had to move into the empty chair, leaving his own chair empty and on someone else's right-hand side.

I had the chair next to me. I began and the exercise went well with the boys saying some useful things to each other and moving seats.

Eventually Mohammed said to the group, 'I think you're all okay. I want you *all* to come and sit next to me!'

And, without hesitation, they did, sitting on each other's knees and draping themselves over each other's shoulders.

I watched, and before this arrangement changed from lopsided human pyramid to fight (the margin for error being small), I sent them back to their chairs.

There were two minutes left. Joel said he wanted both Mohammed and Lemmy to sit next to him because he was gay and wanted to have sex with them.

They both jumped up. Another boy was edged out of his chair. Mohammed and Lemmy sat down on either side of Joel who draped his arms around them in mock affection while they responded with mock excitement.

'There you are!' Joel said to me. 'We're all gay now!'

Through this uneasy kind of humour, I think they were expressing the group's underlying anxiety: the desire for intimacy and the fear of intimacy. This anxiety drives a lot of the daily joking that takes place between young people about being gay and not gay. In most schools, it's difficult for teachers to be openly gay and, as a result, it's almost impossible for students.

A few days before he leaves school, Andrew comes into my counselling room and sits down, sweating slightly. 'I'm going to tell you something I've never told anyone before.'

I feel a mixture of dread and excitement.

His eyes whirl. 'I can hardly say it…' He swallows, hesitates. 'I think I'm gay – well – I *know* I'm gay!'

He looks beseechingly at me, and I feel as if I've just been offered someone's life to look after.

LOVE AND SHAME

Andrew's courage is impressive because young people are more afraid of being shamed than anything else. They'll try to be invisible. They'll make jokes, tease, criticise, bully other people – *anything* to avoid the shameful spotlight being turned on themselves because shame is crippling. Young people are shamed when other people mock their sexuality, laugh at their mistakes, compare them unfavourably with others, criticise the way they look, strip away their privacy or belittle their attempts to look big or cool or clever or attractive. Young people aren't born unconfident, but their confidence gets taken away from them. And they may not do it on purpose but adults often use shame as a way of controlling young people. As a tactic, it works every time because the threat of shame, of being embarrassed in public, will persuade young people to back down and do as they're told.

So I talk about this a lot with young people in counselling. How did you lose your confidence? Who took it away? What happened? At the time, what did you feel like saying to the people involved? Their answers are primed and ready: 'I felt like telling them all to fuck off... I felt like saying, "Well, you're not that great yourself, are you"... I felt like running away... I felt like going and putting a brick through his window... I felt like getting my own back... If I'd had a knife, I'd have killed him!'

Sexual shame leaves an especially bitter legacy. Good sex education may reduce young people's anxiety about sex and need to shame others, but beneath all that the fear of not being loved and of not being loveable is an even greater anxiety.

Erin says she hates her boyfriend. 'He stood there and told me I was a slag in front of all his mates! And when I asked him what I was supposed to have done wrong, he just laughed in my face!' She shakes her head in disbelief. 'God, I hate him so much!'

I ask how long they've been together.

'Too long! We started going out at Natalie's party which was last month so – I don't know – about a month? Something like that. But I don't know what I ever saw in him! I'm never going to speak to him again. He's a complete fucking bastard!'

'What *did* you see in him?'

'Nothing!' Then she stops to think about it. 'Well, I suppose he's quite good looking, if you like that sort of thing. But the trouble is that he knows it, the big-headed bastard!' And, for twenty more minutes, she continues her rant.

It's time for us to end.

'I'm not going to phone him!' she says. 'He'll have to phone me if he wants to speak. I'm not phoning him!'

Erin is hurt and angry because she's been shamed. Underneath everything, she yearns to be loved – really and reliably.

Rhiannon also yearns to be loved but has learned to take nothing for granted. She's been told by her mother that she's fat and ugly so doesn't go home much any more but spends a lot of time at the house where Jezza lives with his girlfriend and their small son. 'He's just a friend,' she tells me earnestly, 'but we get on really well. I know he's a lot older than me but he says he likes having me around.' She watches television with him and makes meals for him when Jezza's girlfriend's at work. 'Don't look at me like that!' she says, grinning wildly. 'There's nothing going on. He wouldn't fancy me anyway!'

Of course she fancies him, I think to myself. But I don't say anything because the fear of some kind of shameful exposure is always present in a counselling room. Will my counsellor see through me? If I tell him something, will he laugh at me? Will he embarrass me? Will he think I'm stupid?

I wait for another young person, Patrick, about whom I've heard terrible, violent things. It's our first counselling appointment and, when he doesn't appear, I go looking for him, my own anxiety rising.

I find him waiting in the wrong place, shuffling about, avoiding my eye. Slung over his shoulder, clearly visible inside its padded, nylon case, is an electric guitar. I feel encouraged. I regularly ask boys, 'What kind of music do you like? Which bands do you like? What's your favourite song?' not dwelling on their replies but making a mental note because they're telling me something personal about themselves. Music is important for so many boys because it says something about power and vulnerability – something they can't say with words but can recognise in drums and guitars, in huge waves of sound like motorbikes, like jet engines on a runway and a plaintive voice buried away somewhere, singing something about love.

'I did it because of what they said about my girlfriend!' says Patrick.

'Your girlfriend?'

'Yeah, well, she's *sort of* my girlfriend. We're going out together, only her parents don't know and we hadn't told anyone yet.'

'Because?'

'I don't know,' he says, embarrassed. 'Because she's younger than me.'

He's fourteen. It emerges that his girlfriend is eleven and the boys he attacked with a baseball bat were making jokes about him and his girlfriend having sex.

'We hadn't even talked about that!' he says, indignantly.

I ask if he's been out with girls before and he says 'not really', meaning 'no'. So this is his first girlfriend and she's eleven. He seems fond of her but other boys have obviously found out and started making jokes about him being a child-molester, upsetting Patrick who probably worries about sex as much as any fourteen-year-old. One advantage of having an eleven-year-old girlfriend is that she's unlikely to be bothered about sex.

So he got the baseball bat, found the boys and hit them with it as many times as possible before being pulled away.

'I don't regret it!' he says. 'I'd do it again!'

'Because you were protecting her?'

'Yeah.'

'Because you love her…'

'I think so.'

I ask him, 'What did you *feel like saying* to them, Patrick? If you could have made them listen, what would you have said?'

He takes some coaxing because he isn't good with words but, slowly, he talks about feeling embarrassed, about it being none of their business, about them laughing and going on and on and on. And about a song he likes. Apparently it's a song about a little man fighting back and earning everyone's respect. 'I'm learning to play it on the guitar,' he says.

LOVE AND PRIVACY

For a young person like Patrick, going out with someone is a public act, fraught with shameful possibilities. Initially, two people are seen spending time together; they're physically affectionate in public. Agreeing to 'go out' is a tacit acknowledgement that, from now on, they're happy to be known as a couple. But the trouble is that going out together is also a very private matter, a matter of intimacy, of something 'that's no one else's business!' Rumours are so alarming and so powerful because they break the skein that exists between our public and private selves.

I've written elsewhere (Luxmoore 2000) about the developmental necessity of young people learning to manage *degrees* of privacy, negotiating a path between absolute openness ('I don't care who knows!') and absolute secrecy ('I don't want anyone to know!'). Romeo and Juliet's tragedy is caused because they can find no middle way between absolute openness and absolute secrecy.

Having a boyfriend or girlfriend dramatises this developmental process. Young people are caught between being independent enough to choose boyfriends and girlfriends for themselves while still being dependent on their parents for food, money and shelter. Bedrooms, for example, typically become the focus of the conflict about privacy in a family with the young person claiming that the bedroom is 'My room and no one else is allowed inside!' It represents absolute personal secrecy. When young people are telling me about the inside of their rooms, it feels as if they're really telling me about the inside of their heads because the way the room's decorated, the way the furniture's arranged, the people who are allowed into the room… these things are so *personal*. Physical changes to the room often mark some personal change in the occupant, saying something about the way the young person is now feeling and how they're now seeing themselves. But despite all this and despite all the protestations, the room still belongs to the parents. They have ultimate control. The ensuing battle over who really controls the room becomes part of a wider battle over who controls the young person's life.

'It's my room!'

'Yes, but it's in my house!'

'So? It's still my room!'

'My room' is where young people can receive their guests and practise hospitality. It's where they can cry, punch the pillow, be naked and daydream.

'I didn't say you could come into my room!'

'I didn't know that I had to ask permission!'

'My room' is where young people can practise being alone and separate from their parents. It's also, potentially, a place to take boyfriends and girlfriends.

'Where are you taking her?'

'Up to my room.'

'Well, I'm sorry, but I don't want the two of you alone in your room.'

'Why not?'

'Because I don't.'

'But why?'

'Because you *know* why!'

And the argument continues, both parties caught between seemingly irreconcilable opposites – parents wanting absolute openness (absolute control) and young people wanting absolute secrecy (absolute control). Old grievances are resurrected:

'You can't tell me what to do!'

'I can while you're living in my house!'

'But that's treating me like a child!'

'Well stop behaving like one, then!'

The battle seems too important to lose. But unless the antagonists can find some way of sharing control, of negotiating an acceptable degree of privacy, things only get worse. A young person might end up secretly arranging something as important as an abortion, for example, because they've reached the point where they feel that they can't tell their parents *anything*, where there's absolutely no room to manoeuvre, where things in the family are either secret or public, where there's no middle ground.

'In a way, I *do* want to tell my mum, but I know she'll tell my dad straightaway and then he'll go ballistic. And then my gran will find out and, before long, the whole world will know!'

'Couldn't you tell her but ask her *not* to tell your dad?'

'I could but she tells him everything! When I first told her about me and Kumar, she went and told him. And when I told her not to read my diary, she waited until I was out of the house and then read it. So I just don't tell her anything any more!'

Counselling affords young people an opportunity to explore what it's like to be neither absolutely secretive nor absolutely open. If the inside of a young person's head is his or her bedroom, then my job is to knock respectfully on the door and wait for an answer. If I'm let in, I don't immediately comment on the state of the room, however filthy or chaotic it might look. I don't open the drawers or look under the bed and I certainly don't inspect the sheets. Instead, I find a place to sit where I can see as much of the room as possible. I ask about the different things I can see and how they came to be in the room. Inevitably, there are leftovers from childhood (a soft toy, a swimming certificate) as well as more recent, daring additions. I treat them with equal interest. When the young person suddenly goes red, jumps up and bundles something away into a cupboard before I can see it, I notice but don't ask. Somebody else may have told me that there's pornography hidden in the box by the CD player, but I let that be. When the young person is ready, he or she may tell me about whatever's in the box, about the soft toy, the swimming certificate and about all the other things in the room. But I let it happen slowly. I may be good at guessing, but I've learned not to rush.

LOVE AND ALONENESS

Young people are often in a mad rush themselves. Life swirls excitedly around, a helter-skelter of parties and noise and expectation. Yet some young people come to my counselling room in a panic because, underneath all the jokes and fun and fooling, the fear of being left alone with no one to love is frightening.

For example, Spencer is a handsome, friendly boy and lots of girls fancy him. Jordan, on the other hand, has freckles and ears that stick out. Jordan gets teased about how he looks and, as a result, hates school. He and I talk together about his recent drinking on the morning bus to school and about how he can get through the next few months in order to leave school with some decent exam results.

I think I know the answer but I want to give him the chance to talk about another important anxiety – his love-life.

He shakes his head. 'Nothing happening. Not interested at the moment, really. Too busy.'

I nod.

A few days later, apparently unprovoked, Jordan breaks Spencer's nose.

Loneliness stalks young people. Winnicott (1965) describes the capacity to be alone as a developmental achievement. Children may be *physically* alone, he argues, but, as long as they've internalised a supportive early relationship, usually with a mother or mothering-figure, they need never feel *emotionally* alone. In my experience, there are young people lacking this capacity to be alone who manage their panic by clinging desperately to friends and, preferably, to as many friends as possible. Even when they're officially going out with someone, their anxiety about being alone never really goes away.

So when two young people break up, the experience is hardest for the person *without* that internalised sense of relationship. For this person, the break-up produces fear and incipient panic. Anxious friends rally round, insisting that the situation is only temporary ('You're bound to find someone!') and only physical ('Remember, you've got us!'). But some young people can take no comfort from these well-meaning reassurances because every break-up is a reminder of a more primitive sense of aloneness where, at the end of the day, other people are *not* waiting with comfort and consolation. The break-up either reinforces that old story ('This always happens! It's the story of my life!') or provides an opportunity to reconsider whether that story is as inevitable as it seems ('At least this time it was me who dumped *her*! At least this time I don't care!')

Ronan was going out with Maeve for longer than with any of his other girlfriends but he tells me that their relationship has just ended.

I ask how he's feeling.

'I don't care!' he says. 'I hate her!'

And despite all my attempts to help him think about the good as well as the bad in the relationship, he insists that hate is all he feels.

I ask about things at home.

He hates his parents as well, he says. 'Especially my mum. She's a bitch!'

In previous conversations, he's never exactly enthused about his mother but the fact that he's now claiming to hate her at the same time as hating Maeve suggests a connection. His mother and Maeve used to get on really well, he adds. They used to watch lots of television together. Apparently, the break-up came after Maeve said Ronan was childish. Whether or not she actually said this, it sounds more like the complaint of a parent than a girlfriend and I wonder how much his mother and Maeve have become interchangeable in Ronan's mind; how much the break-up with Maeve echoes an old sense of separation from his mother, an abiding sense of being alone in the world, unloved by her. Hatred may be Ronan's way of dealing with this, his best defence (see Chapter 3). He's probably always hated being alone.

But it's the end of the day, our appointment is about to end and Ronan is fidgeting, anxious to find his friends in case they go home without him.

LOVE AND FRIENDS

Anna is also anxious about losing her friends. She comes to see me because she doesn't know what to do. 'We've been friends for ages – in fact, since the first year at this school – but now it feels like nobody in our group wants to do anything together any more...' She traces this feeling back to the time when Paige first started going out with Morgan.

I think there's always a sense in which two young people going out together are also going out with each other *on behalf of the others*. The two of them have a private relationship with each other but their relationship is also public property: other people know about it and it has an effect on those people – not only on family members but also on friends and sometimes on a wider group of peers, all of whom have an investment in the new couple's relationship.

The couple become the focus of much salacious interest... Are they right for each other? Are they behaving in the way we expect couples to behave and, above all, are they *doing it*? Most groups initially pretend to be unconcerned ('It's no big deal! It's their business!') but are perfectly well aware of what's happening and are watching, watching. Some groups are watching in order to learn, watching the movement of bodies and strategically placed hands as the couple sit nearby, self-consciously entwined. Other groups make no secret of their fascination ('Have you had her yet?') but distance themselves from any rebounding accusations ('Just because no one wants to have sex with you!') by caricaturing their interest. For example, once a boy starts going out with a girl, the remaining boys in the group immediately step up their level of heterosexual banter. They punch each other and play-fight. They sit further apart from each other and start boasting of immense sexual accomplishments because the existence of this new couple reminds them that *they're all boys*, which raises their homophobic anxiety and their anxiety about being alone.

The lovers offer the group all sorts of projective possibilities. They can represent group anxieties about intimacy, performance, sex and sexuality, which leak out all the time in speculation, gossip and joking about the two people. But there are other, unspoken issues. What exactly does this mean for us as a group? Does our friend care more for his new girlfriend than he cares for us? Will our group change because of this?

The group usually sets the couple a loyalty test. The rest of the group are 'all going' somewhere and, under normal circumstances, everyone would be expected to go. The lovers are left with a choice between doing what they'd originally planned to do as a couple or doing what the group expects them to do. There's usually no room for compromise, and relationships can change fundamentally, depending on the couple's decision.

The group claims that this test is only for the couple ('He's got to choose between her and us!') but there are usually other things going on. A group that's stuck – where the relationships have become fixed, the roles inflexible, each person obliged to be the way they've always been in the group – will be looking for a way out of the impasse. So the fact that one member of the group has a new loyalty and may be in the process of leaving the group gives everybody else an opportunity to realign themselves. And with any change, there are knock-on effects: other people can try out new roles and sub-groupings or the group may seize the opportunity to disband altogether, blaming the couple ('It's not the same any more!') while feeling secretly relieved that the lovers have provoked this long-overdue change.

This may be what's happened in Anna's group. Unconsciously, they may all have been looking for a way of changing things after so many years together. Paige and Morgan may simply have made that change possible. Anna may be left feeling sad but other members of the group may be quietly relieved.

It emerges from our conversation that, even though Anna was fond of the other members of the group, Paige had always been her best friend. Anna knew perfectly well that Paige liked Morgan and understood perfectly well that Paige had every right to go out with whomsoever she chose. Indeed, even now, part of Anna is happy for her friend. But another part of her has been hurt by her best friend's new relationship, and that's what we'll talk about in counselling until Anna can find a way of loving her friend while letting her go.

LOVE AND LOSS

This will be as hard for Anna as it is for any young person. Most of the pop songs ever written have been about breaking up because, when it happens, it feels as if part of a person has been lost, has been amputated. It hurts *that* much. Kohut (1971) describes a self as made up of 'selfobjects' – relationships with other people which give us an identity, which become parts of who we are. It may be that we fall in love with the person without whom our sense of self is incomplete, and so losing that person months or years later feels like losing a part of our selves.

For young people, therefore, breaking up with a serious boyfriend or girlfriend is momentous. Romeo and Juliet can't live without each other. Usain's panicking because the girl he loves has just ended their relationship. 'I don't know what to do!' he says. 'I don't know whether go round and see her or whether to phone her. I don't know whether to ask for another chance. I can't stop thinking about her. And it's come at the worst possible time because I'm about to start university!'

He wants to talk about her and we do, remembering the good and the not-so-good times. But all the while, like a detective, he's hunting for clues.

'I know I haven't seen so much of her lately but that's because I've been working and she knows that. It's hardly a reason to break up with me!'

I ask what he's feeling about going to university.

'Mixed,' he says. 'Looking forward to it, obviously. But I don't know what it's going to be like being away from home for so long. And I don't know what the other people are going to be like because I've been put into a flat with nine other people I don't know.'

And, with that, we return to his girlfriend. Without her, he loses his confidence, his best friend, the voice on the phone, the person who replies to his texts.

Without her, university looms very large.

My job is to help young people live through the sadnesses and satisfactions, the transitions of growing up without being destroyed when things go wrong. I help to bear the load, making it possible for the two of us to keep thinking together, even when strong feelings threaten to overwhelm us. But, inevitably, promises *do* get broken and people *do* get hurt. There are times when I sit with a young person, knowing that nothing can change in the foreseeable future and that, for the moment, life really does feel wretched.

'I don't want to break up with him!' pleads Sophie. 'There must be *something* I can do? I love him!'

She does love him. I know she does because I've listened to her talking about him for weeks – her happiness when they started going out together, holding hands, kissing for the first time. I've listened to her talking about how proud she felt to have such a wonderful boyfriend and her increasing belief that this wasn't just a fluke.

And now he's told her – in the nicest possible way – that it's over.

She stares at me, *willing* me to do something, to make it different, to make him come back.

I say that I'm really, really sorry.

She looks away, angry, scared. And heartbroken.

3

Young People in Hate

Outside it was dark – trees shivering, birds silent, a few cars parked under streetlights, away from any shadows. But the curfew had passed and everyone was safely inside the Youth Centre now with coloured lights flashing, the dance floor busy, the walls beginning to sweat, people shouting to be heard above the music and at least one toilet already blocked. With less than an hour to go, dozens of young people who'd been dancing, flirting, fooling and passing messages to each other all night were beginning to pair off – shuffling closer, negotiating arms and legs, inquisitive hands and kisses as the disco moved towards its denouement, the bit that really mattered, the slow songs.

I went outside to make sure that no one was around, drinking or drunk, causing trouble or lying in wait for any of the happy couples who might eventually emerge into the night. As a team of youth workers, we always did this, patrolling a large area outside and beyond the Youth Centre in order to keep the disco safe, making sure that nobody outside could spoil whatever was going on inside.

I wandered away towards the tennis courts, out of sight of the Youth Centre. On nights like these, there would often be young people hanging around in the shadows, bored and wanting to chat ('We hate discos! Why can't you organise something *good?*) or maudlin and drunk, bewailing some misfortune. Most would be minding their own business but occasionally someone would be smashing bottles, throwing stones or plotting against someone in the Youth Centre. So, once the curfew had passed, we insisted on moving anyone choosing to remain outside the Youth Centre as far away from it as possible.

Three figures loomed into view.

I headed towards them, expecting to chat briefly before gently shooing them off.

There were two smaller, younger boys I knew slightly and one much bigger boy whom I knew extremely well. At seventeen, Vinnie was already taller and stronger than me or any of the other youth workers. We built our annual Youth Centre tug-of-war team around him. He won every bored, impromptu arm-wrestling competition and, because of his size and strength, was generally reckoned to be a person with whom you didn't mess. Whenever word went round that a carload of idiots from another town were coming to beat someone up, Vinnie was called and quickly came to everyone's rescue. I liked him. He contributed a lot to the Youth Centre, helping with the younger age groups and enjoying himself – a gentle giant once you got to know him.

The younger boys said hello but Vinnie seemed grumpy, distracted. I asked if the three of them were just passing through.

'Why? What's it got to do with you?'

'I'm just asking, Vinnie. I'm asking because you need to move further away from the Youth Centre.'

'Why?'

'Because we've got a disco going on and you know we don't have people hanging around outside at night.'

'So?'

'So I need you to move on.'

'And what are you going to do?' He came towards me.

This wasn't like him. I wondered if he was drunk. 'You just need to move these guys away. If the three of you are hanging around and anything happens, you could get accused of something you didn't do.'

'Like what?'

'I don't know! Look, you know the score, Vinnie.'

But, for some reason, he didn't know the score. 'Fuck off, Nick!'

'Vinnie, you need to take these guys away...'

'Yeah?' He came and stood right in front of me, pushing his face into mine. 'What are you going to do about it?'

I was about to be head-butted. I felt scared, trying to decide whether to back away from this confrontation (probably the sensible, health-and-safety thing to do) or challenge his behaviour and risk being hit.

I held my breath, unable to move, feeling stupid, feeling scared.

He'd made his point. Sneering, he backed off, shouting that he fucking hated me, that I couldn't tell him what to do and that I could go and fuck the Youth Centre.

But he and the two boys were walking away.

I said nothing, stuck on auto-pilot, trying my best to look brave and unperturbed but thinking, 'Vinnie was about to beat me up! I've known him since he was eleven! We've been camping, swimming, skating – loads of stuff. We've spent hours talking together in the Youth Centre and he was about to beat me up!'

HATRED AND EVIL

This chapter is about hatred. Young people are constantly saying that they hate things and it's a word I sometimes get asked *not* to use by adults on training courses.

'I think you mean frustration,' they say, 'or maybe anger... Hate's too strong.'

'No,' I say, 'I mean hate.'

'But hate doesn't really exist,' they say. 'Would you mind not using it?'

I think that hatred exists as surely as love exists and needs to be understood or it becomes frightening and unmentionable. In my experience, a lot of young people's hatred remains unconscious, expressed obliquely in ways I'll describe, whereas other young people like Vinnie express their hatred overtly, becoming frightening and unmentionable themselves unless we can bear the fact that young people really do – from time to time – hate.

Part of the problem is that hatred gets confused with evil which – whether it exists or not – is popularly reckoned to be the preserve of paedophiles, murderers and genocidal dictators. Lionel Shriver's (2005) novel *We Need to Talk about Kevin* tells the story of a fourteen-year-old who has rounded up a selection of his peers and one teacher, locked them in the school Sports Hall and then, quite deliberately, shot them dead. Kevin is now in prison for life and isn't sorry.

Shriver's novel explores a thousand possible explanations for Kevin's behaviour: his family and his childhood – inevitably – and lots more. Nothing is resolved. There are glimmerings of understanding but always a sense that perhaps some people are just *like that*. Perhaps loving our children *isn't* enough.

I've only ever worked with one person like Kevin. He didn't lose his temper. In fact, he was very rational. He bullied, for sure; he got into trouble at school – all the usual things. But there was a coldness about him. Not a withdrawn, unhappy kind of coldness but something hard, unflinching. In counselling we maintained a superficially friendly relationship, but I knew I was never getting close. We talked about his family and childhood but made no emotional connection either in thinking about these things or with each other. He left school, beat somebody up and went to prison.

Writing about war criminals, Arendt (1963) famously describes 'the banality of evil' – behaviour which is utterly deliberate and utterly careless. I think it's important not to confuse young people's hatred with the brute indifference of someone like Kevin. I've worked with plenty of young people who have done bad things. I once taught a boy in school and then, a few years later, found myself teaching him again in prison! But he was basically warm-hearted. There was nothing sinister about him. Spinelli (2001) describes evil as 'acts committed through indifference, through arrogance and error of judgement and through purposeful intent' (p.114). Whatever we mean by 'evil' involves making some kind of moral choice, whereas hatred can't be helped. It's normal. It's the very opposite of indifference. Hatred exists only where relationships exist. The young people I worked with when I was a youth worker weren't evil, and the young people I work with now as a counsellor aren't evil. But they do hate. So this chapter is an attempt to understand what young people mean when they talk about hating things and what might have been going on inside Vinnie on the night of the disco.

HATRED AND MOTHERING

There are different ways of understanding hatred, and all of them involve love. Klein (1935/1975) describes the way a baby begins its life in blissfully merged harmony with its mother. The mother loves her baby and the baby loves her. She responds whenever the baby cries. But soon the baby realises that there are times when it cries, when it's unhappy, when it needs something and she *doesn't* come running. So the baby concludes that it must have two mothers – a good one who's around some of the time and a bad one who appears at other times: a loveable, 'gratifying' mother and a hateful, 'frustrating' one. Klein describes the baby in this early, primitive state as both loving and hating its mother and struggling (indeed, struggling for the rest of its life) to come to terms with the fact that these two mothers are one and the same person and that its feelings towards her are, in fact, mixed.

Klein's idea is that we can't help but internalise this first loving-and-hating relationship and it becomes the blueprint upon which all our other relationships are based. In other words, we end up seeing the world and everything in it – unconsciously – as a vast and varied 'mother' who can sometimes be wonderful, making us feel so good, while at other times, she can seem heartless and make us feel so bad.

More than anything else, my work as a counsellor with young people is about helping them to bear this struggle: the struggle between loving and hating an internalised, unconscious 'mother' and, by extension, the evolving, daily struggle to come to terms with the imperfection of other people and the world out there. It's a struggle that affects everything, taking us all back to where we started as babies – sad, disappointed and furious that the good mother seemed to have gone off-duty and the bad one returned. 'Why, oh why can't the good one stay? Why can't the bad one go away and never come back? Why can't she just get lost?'

Young people are living with the daily disappointment of this. So rather than begin counselling with all the things that are going well and that they love about their lives, they typically begin with a miscellany of hates: 'I hate my hair! I hate Maths! I hate this weather! I hate it when people are two-faced! I hate school! I hate being told what to do! I hate my sister…!' It's as if the great bird of hatred is forever flying around, looking for somewhere – anywhere – to land.

It's easy to dismiss so much over-statement, so much striving for effect. Of course, hatred is far too strong a word to describe the irritation, powerlessness and disappointment young people feel. Of course they don't really hate their hair or Maths. But they do have a sense of hating *something*, even if they can't quite put their finger on it… Shaquille says he hates thinking about the boys who bullied him. Kelly hates her dance teacher who's told her to lose weight. Bud's view of the world is coloured by the extreme dyslexia which means he must sit through hour after hour of school, week after week, without ever making much progress. He hates school. Sarah hates having to do all the worst jobs in the hair salon where she works. James can't accept the fact that Kimberley doesn't love him any more and really *is* going out with someone else. He hates himself, he says.

Although our first relationship is with an actual mother, the hatred stomping around in a person's unconscious as he or she grows older no longer refers to a literal mother ('my mum') but to a generalised sense of *mothering*, a sense of being (or not being) recognised, looked after and cherished by whoever's around – male or female, father or mother, friend or foe. Young people like Shaquille, Kelly, Bud, Sarah and James are likely to complain about things being unfair because underneath everything, *unconsciously*, they're also dealing with the unfairness of mother-figures being less than perfect while on the surface, *consciously*, that sense of unfairness is focused on other things.

Their hatred often gets expressed obliquely. Naomi doesn't necessarily tell me about hating people or even about things being unfair, despite being obliged to listen to her mum and step-dad fighting downstairs every night. Rather than complain, rather than scream, she keeps quiet for fear of making the situation worse and, sitting alone in her bedroom, cuts herself.

She shows me the scars up and down her arms. 'If I could, I'd get rid of them all,' she says, 'except for three. I'd keep the one from when my grandad died and the one from when my mum took an overdose and the one from when I had the abortion.'

Weeks later, for the first time in her life, she gets excluded from school for swearing at a teacher and, because the alternative was probably another cut on her arm, I tell her that, as her counsellor, I'm glad.

She laughs.

I ask her what she'd *really* like to say to people, especially to her mum and step-dad. And little by little she begins, hesitant at first, struggling with words, worried in case swearing isn't allowed in counselling but growing more and more confident, telling me what she, Naomi, really, really feels about other people's behaviour. Telling her hatred, *really* telling it and sensing that it's been heard is better than turning it against herself and, in particular, against her arms.

Kenzie finds it easier than Naomi to talk about hating. He begins with a story about his ex-girlfriend, Rachel. 'I hate her!' he says. 'I really do! I'm better off without her!'

Apparently, she kissed another boy at a party and then denied it when Kenzie heard about what had happened from other people at the party.

'She's such a slag! I never trusted her. When we were going out, she was always getting texts from other blokes and she said she didn't like it but you could see she did... God, I fucking hate her!'

I suspect that young people tell so many hating stories about being betrayed by boyfriends and girlfriends (and they do!) because the experience reminds them of a much more powerful sense of betrayal (Hillman 1964) by a once-perfect, all-loving mother who sometimes went off and left them and who evidently loved other people as well. Young people hate feeling betrayed by anyone. They hate the thought that it might happen again and they experience most relationship break-ups as betrayals of some sort.

Stories like Kenzie's are usually ways of practising talking about something more important, ways of warming up to the real story. In Kenzie's case, the person who matters most isn't Rachel but his mother.

However, he moves on to talking about his father next. 'I hate my dad! The other day he knew perfectly well that I'd just split up with Rachel but he went on and on, saying that I should get over her and there's plenty more fish in the sea. I know he was trying to be helpful but he wasn't. So I told him to fuck off and we ended up having a massive row with him threatening to kick me out and telling me that if I didn't like living with him then I should go and live with my mum!'

I ask if that's possible.

'No way! Especially not after what happened with my sister!'

Kenzie's mother is an alcoholic. One day, her boyfriend (also an alcoholic) hit Kenzie's sister so hard that he broke her arm. When Alys told her mother what had happened, her mother accused her of lying, got some water and a bar of soap and attempted to clean out Alys's mouth by forcing soap into it.

Kenzie heard about what had happened and, armed with a baseball bat, went round to his mother's house intending to kill her boyfriend. He couldn't get in so he broke some windows and came away again. The police arrested him later that day.

Other professionals are now involved with the family but Kenzie and I will keep talking about the mixture of things he feels – protective and vengeful, kind and cruel. This conversation was rehearsed in our earlier conversation about his ex-girlfriend Rachel – the slag, the person he could never trust. In talking about her, he described feeling furious, deserted, betrayed. He resolved never to trust her again. The parallels between his ex-girlfriend and his mother are clear.

Of course, mothers make mistakes and Kenzie's mother may have made more than her fair share. But Kenzie doesn't love and hate her because she's an unreliable alcoholic who once used to be reliable and sober. He loves and hates her *because she's his mother* – simple as that. Her recent behaviour only dramatises for Kenzie a primitive, unconscious and unfolding dialogue between love and hate, between a fair and an unfair world which is continually being played out and evolving in young people's minds. As a result, their moods fluctuate. They can be madly in love one week, planning whole lives together, then madly in hate the next, threatening each other with whatever cruelties come to mind.

And living with these erratic moods can be hard work for other people. Because of their moodiness and changing behaviour (sleeping late, saying less, not wanting to join in with the family), dozens of young people are taken off by their worried parents to see the doctor. Suddenly, there's talk of psychiatric assessments.

I ask about their visits to the doctor.

'She just asked me questions about what I like doing and stuff.'

'Was that all?'

'And how I was getting on at school. But I didn't really say anything.'

I picture the poor doctor, expected to treat a bad dose of adolescence, knowing that there's probably an underlying family angle on this which he or she is never going to be told about – rows between the parents, one of them having an affair or having problems at work, middle-aged life losing its sparkle. A stroppy son or daughter is offered up as the presenting problem. But doctors have to be careful. They also know that some young people do get depressed and that psychiatric problems can start young. So they hedge their bets. They talk about the possibility of someone doing a psychiatric assessment but suggest waiting a bit longer to see how things develop.

This excites and scares everyone. I ask what's going to happen next.

'Don't know really. She said to go back if I want but, to be honest, I can't see the point.'

Hamlet's parents worry about their son. People say he's 'mad' but no one can be sure how or why. They only know that he's behaving strangely. Is he in love? Is he in hate? Desperate to understand, they conclude that he must be upset about his father's death.

It's traditional in Shakespearean studies to describe Hamlet as indecisive, meditating on the underlying purpose of life because he can't make up his mind whether or not to take revenge for his father's death. His famous 'to be or not to be' speech is usually interpreted as meaning 'to take action or not to take action' or as 'to live or not to live'. I think it's helpful to think of him as someone caught between loving and hating. This state of mind feels like a madness to Hamlet as he tries, like any young person, to make sense of such contradictory feelings. On the one hand, he loves his mother but, on the other hand, hates her for what she's done, marrying so soon after his father's death. He hates her vulnerability, her neediness. He hates her for having sex with her new husband. And all of this infects his relationship with his girlfriend who gets tarred with the same brush. Hamlet rages at Ophelia and she doesn't understand. One minute he's rude, off-hand and cruel to her and the next he's tender and conciliatory the way he used to be. This emotional confusion (Does he love me? Does he hate me?) drives her mad while Hamlet is living with a different kind of madness – the madness of mixed feelings, the madness of ambivalence:

...in my heart there was a kind of fighting
That would not let me sleep.

Hamlet, Act 5, Scene 2

If Klein is right and a baby – unable to reflect and think about itself – necessarily splits its mother into two mothers – a good, satisfying one and a bad, unsatisfying one – then Hamlet's problem is that, unlike a baby, he *can* reflect and *can* think about himself and must therefore hold these opposites to be true, however difficult that may be. Like any young person, he must come to terms with the fact that his mother is both good and bad, strong and weak, loyal and disloyal. He must come to terms with the fact that he can't simplify and split her into *only* good or *only* bad and can't – by extension – believe his step-father to be wholly bad, whatever wickedness his step-father may have done.

If he was unable to think about these opposites, it would be easier for Hamlet to kill his step-father. He would simply grab the nearest weapon. But, to his credit, he can think ('I will speak daggers to her, but use none'), he can contemplate these opposites and so, instead, he teases, taunts, derides, jokes, agonises, mocks, confuses, philosophises... Like so many young people, his hatred gets muddled up with his love and can't be enacted straightforwardly. It seeps out in these perplexing ways.

There are plenty of other ways. Rio uses drugs. Lots of them. They chill him out, he says. They soothe him like a mother soothes her baby, making the bad feelings go away. 'When I'm feeling stressy, I get mashed. I reckon I'm spoiling myself with ganja like my mum used to spoil me with treats. I know it's pointless but I do it anyway.'

Estelle uses sex. Not deliberately – she doesn't plan it – but sex and the pursuit of sex distract her from feelings about her parents. Sex staves off depression, making her feel alive, connected with other human beings. But because she has sex with so many boys, she's shunned by the girls who used to be her friends. It's as if she takes her hatred out on herself, punishing herself with unprotected, loveless sex, losing all her friends but claiming, all the while, to hold no grudges and to be fond of everyone. I think Estelle is full of hatred but she smiles and smiles and smiles... Until she can keep it up no longer and takes an overdose.

And in addition to Estelle and Rio, there are young people who steal, who starve themselves and use all manner of other behaviours to defend against primitive, unconscious hatred. Schools are often on the receiving end of this behaviour.

'I hate school,' says Luke, not angrily but matter-of-factly.

Plenty of young people say that they hate school but they say it to make an impression; they say it with force; they say it with swearing.

Luke is almost nonchalant, adding that he hates the headteacher – but not vehemently, not glaring at me to make sure that I realise just how strongly he feels. Instead, it's more of an afterthought. 'When he shouts at me, I just laugh and he hates that.'

Luke spends a lot of time in isolation, sitting in the corridor, barred from lessons as punishment for his misbehaviour, pretending to do Maths or English. He says he likes being in isolation because he gets to talk to all the people going past, including his friends.

Suddenly, I have a Clever Counsellor's idea and ask if being in isolation is easy because that's how he's always been in his life.

He doesn't understand.

'I was wondering if you've always felt on your own, Luke – cut off from other people?'

'No,' he says, 'I've never felt that. I don't care about being in isolation.'

So much for Clever Counsellors' ideas! Sometimes they're right but usually their timing is wrong. Luke remains an enigma and the more I try to crack the code, the more he deflects, defends and the more stupid I feel. Yet despite me being a Clumsy Counsellor, he's surprisingly friendly. We get on well and I realise that what he probably needs most from me is a relationship – not clever psychological insights. Later on in our relationship I'll learn that he's never lived with his father; that his father is in and out of prison, convicted of shocking things; that Luke has never really known what to make of his father's existence and that being matter-of-fact, nonchalant and apparently unconcerned is his way of dealing with a father from whom he really *is* isolated. 'I don't care' makes absolute sense because if he *did* care he'd be hurt, angry, confused, sad. I suspect that 'school' becomes a father-figure for him as it becomes a kind of parent-figure for most young people (Luxmoore 2008). When the headteacher engages with Luke, argues with him, cares about him, gets frustrated with him, Luke doesn't know how to react. So he laughs because it would be dangerous to take 'school' or any other father-figure seriously.

From time to time in our work together, we talk about the biological father he doesn't know, the father he currently imagines as a vaguely disapproving, punitive kind of school. In the meantime, we continue our relationship and, at least within that, he's not in isolation.

Just as the idea of a 'school' focuses primitive, unconscious feelings of love and hate for young people like Luke, so, too, does the idea of a youth centre – a youth centre with a disco raging inside and Vinnie glaring at me in the darkness, out by the tennis courts.

HATRED AND DEPENDENCY

I've thought a lot about what happened with Vinnie that night. Grumpy and bored, he may simply have been showing off to the two younger boys. Or his behaviour may have been triggered by alcohol. His breath certainly smelled of booze, which may have released an aggression he normally kept locked away inside his 'big friendly giant' persona. Or it may have been that, challenged by an authority-figure – however gently – he suddenly transferred on to me feelings about other authority-figures in his life and, for fifteen frighteningly long seconds, I became his hated father or step-mother.

These theories may be true. But I've also wondered how much Vinnie's behaviour was related to what was going on inside the Youth Centre, inside *his* Youth Centre...

At the time, he wasn't going out with anyone, unlike most of his friends. He'd never been out with anyone. He wasn't especially good-looking but I suspect that it was his size which made it harder for him to be taken seriously as boyfriend material. For a girl, it would have meant going out with a giant rather than with one of his smaller, sleekly oiled, less daunting sidekicks. And, for another boy, going out with Vinnie would have meant standing out, not only as gay, but as enormously gay! Being small can be difficult for boys (Luxmoore 2006), but being bigger than anyone else brings its own problems. Whatever he happened to be doing at the time, Vinnie would have felt obliged to go and stand as a deterrent whenever the out-of-town idiots came over. He would have felt obliged to take part in the tug-of-war competitions, the arm-wrestling. He would have felt obliged to laugh at jokes about horses' penises, the Incredible Hulk, the Eiffel Tower.

I've wondered how much he was unconsciously aware – outside, in the darkness of the tennis courts – of all the other young people inside the Youth Centre, flirting with each other and dancing, laughing with each other and touching. He'd been to plenty of discos himself, rarely dancing because his size made him clumsy but staying in the shadows, watching. He knew what went on and I imagine he'd felt increasingly awkward as he'd got older, longing for some kind of romantic contact. Suttie (1935) writes, 'Hatred... owes all its meaning to a demand for love' (p.37).

I've wondered whether he was gay. Perhaps he was hiding from a homophobic world by performing feats of seemingly heterosexual machismo. To have asked him would have risked everything. Young people have told me that they're gay, but I've never asked unless a young person has very obviously led the conversation in that direction. Some young people simply don't know whether they're gay and others aren't ready to talk about it. So until I know for sure, I try to avoid making assumptions about 'girls' and 'boys' but refer, instead, to 'people' and 'partners'. That way, a young person doesn't have to start counselling by pretending to be heterosexual.

I decided that to punish Vinnie for his behaviour without talking to him first would be unfair. He'd certainly scared me, and I was sure he'd been close to head-butting me. But for all I knew, he might have scared himself and might now be sorry. His behaviour that night might well have been provoked by something which had nothing to do with me.

I phoned the next day.

'I don't really want to talk about it,' he said, 'and I'm probably not going to be coming back to the Youth Centre again, anyway!'

This much was predictable. Knowing that they've done something wrong and feeling embarrassed, young people often run from situations, claiming not to care. They *do* care, but sometimes it feels safer to end the relationship altogether than to face the embarrassment of apologising.

I said that I'd be very sorry if he didn't come to the Youth Centre again and that we needed to talk about what had happened. I encouraged him to come and see me later that day.

He said he'd think about it.

Nothing happened. There was no sign of him later that day or the next.

I decided that waiting for him to come to me wasn't an option. Unless I made the running, he'd never come back; he'd be expecting to be banned from the Youth Centre and would be feeling ashamed. So I went round to his house.

He opened the door. 'Oh, yeah…'

No one else seemed to be in. The television stayed on.

I asked how he was.

'Okay. Sorry about the other night, by the way.'

I said I wanted to understand more about what had happened.

He tried to brush it off. 'I was pissed off, you know? I'd had a drink. I don't know what was the matter with me… Sorry, okay?'

'It felt like you were about to head-butt me, Vinnie.'

'Did it? Yeah, I'm sorry. You know I'm not really like that.'

I agreed with him. 'So what was pissing you off?'

'Usual things… My dad, my step-mum.'

I wondered whether I *had* temporarily become someone else in his unconscious. But if I'd become his dad or step-mum, nagging at him to do something he didn't want to do, then why not just have an argument with me? Why not refuse to budge and maybe swear at me a bit? Why come so close to violence and to what felt – albeit briefly – like hatred?

'How come you weren't at the disco?'

'I'm bored of discos. They're always the same.'

'You mean, people getting off with each other…?'

'Something like that.'

I wondered whether it hurt to go to discos because he imagined no one would ever want to get off with him, but at the same time it hurt not to go because then there was absolutely no chance. Perhaps the tennis courts marked a painful kind of limbo: close to the disco and to the possibility of romance but also cut off from that possibility. Kernberg (1992) writes about hatred as a defence against dependency, a protection against the vulnerability of needing something and not being able to get it so that, in effect, a person is saying, *If I can't have the thing I need, the thing I long for, then I'll hate that need and crush that longing.* Lots of young people would share Vinnie's predicament and react in a similar way, avoiding something with the potential to embarrass or hurt. Perhaps he was drawn to the disco, longing to be part of it but hating it for the vulnerability it left him feeling and hating me as its representative, come to expose him, wandering around in limbo by the tennis courts. I wondered about the meaning of our faces so close together – close enough to head-butt and close enough to kiss – perhaps enacting something of his hostility and longing, his hatred and love in the same unwitting way that boys do when they threaten each other, saying, 'I could *have* you!' And it may be far-fetched but I also wondered whether, in telling me to go and fuck the Youth Centre, he imagined I was metaphorically able to do what he had no opportunity to do.

Sexual loneliness is humiliating for young people. In playground cultures boys are forever calling each other 'wanker' and I'm at pains to reassure them in sex education lessons that 'Everyone does it – girls do it as well and guys usually do it a lot. Don't believe any man who tells you that he's never had a wank!' It seems important to say this (and they seem reassured) because the shame surrounding masturbation means that it's still a significant insult, albeit hurled by one wanker at another. I think it's the *needing* that young people hate. Boy wankers scorn other boy wankers who remind them of their own need. Masturbation succeeds by getting rid of the need and the longing, and returns us to an independent, autonomous state, back in control.

Like anyone, Vinnie was vulnerable because of his need, and hating was perhaps his fiercest way of disguising that need, that vulnerability. Sitting in his living room, I wondered what I could possibly say to acknowledge any of this without exposing his vulnerability. As with Luke and his imagined father, institutions become mother-like or father-like. Whether they're schools, hospitals or – in Vinnie's case – a youth centre, we experience them as unconscious reminders of an original mothering we've loved and hated. As we grow older, we tell ourselves an evolving story about that mothering (she loved me, she didn't love me, I loved her, I didn't love her, she tried to love me, she did her best…) and institutions become the unwitting focus of that process. At an unconscious level, we approve or disapprove of them in terms of the mothering they do or don't seem to provide. Inevitably, Vinnie had strong feelings about the Youth Centre as a mothering-figure, as a collection of relationships. After all, it had looked after him since he was eleven. It had been pleased to see him, week after week, enjoying his company, helping him to make friends when he was younger, keeping his secrets, taking him on trips, telling him off and forgiving him. He had loyally returned its affection and was beginning to take some responsibility for its younger children.

But like anyone trying to construct a mothering story, his feelings about the Youth Centre were mixed. Sometimes things go well and we feel well-disposed towards our mother-figures (she loves me) but, at other times, life seems unfair, things go wrong, people misunderstand, we don't get what we deserve and we blame an internalised mother-figure (she loves me not). Tolerating this paradoxical mixture of strong feelings is a developmental achievement which most people only manage as they get older. In the meantime, the feeling that she isn't there or isn't fair is awful. So we set out to destroy the feeling. The logic goes that *If only I can stop needing her, then the bad feelings will go away and I'll never be disappointed again because I'll never allow myself to have another relationship in which I'm vulnerable.* This strategy (never consciously chosen but evolving as an unconscious response to a frightening situation) is what Kernberg (1970) calls 'malignant narcissism' – an inability or refusal to enter into empathic relationships.

Kernberg's idea about hatred as a defence against dependency (Vinnie's need for love causing him momentarily to hate) is based on an understanding of the way a child develops and the difference between normal, 'primary' narcissism (Freud 1914) and malignant narcissism. The theory goes that a baby is born, unable to differentiate between itself and its mother. The baby is everything and everything is the baby. This developmental stage is called 'primary narcissism', the baby seeing itself in everything and seeing everything as an extension of itself. But slowly the baby learns that other people are separate and exist in their own right. It learns that they're not extensions of itself, that it can't control them but must enter into relationships with them.

This is a crucial learning process. It may take years finally to accept the existence and autonomy of other people. Kernberg's malignant narcissism describes what happens when a baby (or child or young person) fails to make this transition and goes on believing that everyone and everything is only an extension of itself. Symington (1993) writes, 'In the narcissistic illusion there is no other; there is only me... One of the ways in which I sustain the delusion that there is no other is to control this other' (p.86). The baby becomes the child who becomes the young person who goes on expecting to control the world. So when someone or something refuses to be controlled, the narcissistic young person, unable to enter into the subtle give-and-take of relationships, has no way of dealing with this. The narcissist hates the experience because it challenges the illusion that he or she controls everybody. He or she resorts to violence in order to kill off this hated part of the self which, for some reason, is refusing to do as it's told. Fonagy (2004) describes violence as a form of self-defence, because violence seems to be the only way of shoring up the narcissistic self, desperately putting back defences which appear to have been breached by an intruder expecting a give-and-take relationship.

In a famous novel, a small boy 'starving, and houseless, and as good as dumb' is scooped up from the streets of Liverpool where 'Not a soul knew to whom it belonged...'. Sullen and already 'hardened... to ill-treatment', the boy is taken off to a middle-class home where he is physically and repeatedly bullied by the son of the household whom, not surprisingly, he grows to hate. People say that the boy's hatred is because of his 'violent nature' but, to the boy, hatred makes sense. He plots revenge against the son of the household because 'while I'm thinking of that, I don't feel pain'.

This is Heathcliff in Emily Brontë's *Wuthering Heights*, a novel more obviously about hatred than about love; a novel exploring whether hatred is caused by nature or nurture. In films, Heathcliff grows into a brooding, handsome romantic hero, but in the novel itself things are much darker. In the novel, his behaviour is affected by what's happened to him as a child and his life thereafter is dedicated to revenge. He only manages to make one affectionate relationship in his life, and that relationship is entirely co-dependent, as if both people were extensions of each other. Catherine is wholly identified with him, 'I *am* Heathcliff', while for Heathcliff, 'existence, after losing her, would be hell'. She's the only person who penetrates his narcissistic, hating shell and she dies, aged only nineteen. He's one year older. Feeling abandoned by her (perhaps as he was abandoned on the streets of Liverpool), Heathcliff dedicates himself to keeping her memory alive as if she were still a part of himself. He shuts out everyone else.

Eighteen years later, before he dies, his niece asks him, 'Have you never loved *anybody*, in all your life, uncle? *Never?*'

He answers that he has only ever loved Catherine:

> I cannot look down to this floor, but her features are shaped on the flags! In every cloud, in every tree – filling the air at night, and caught by glimpses in every object by day, I am surrounded with her image! The most ordinary faces of men and women – my own features – mock me with a resemblance.

Hollywood might deem this romantic. Others might describe it as narcissistically disturbed. Perhaps it's both. Perhaps Heathcliff hates and tries to control people because people keep trying to have relationships with him and his only way of staying safe from the threat of their unreliable love is to keep them all under brutal, callous control.

Heathcliff may be at the 'malignant' end of Kernberg's narcissistic continuum but I think that most people have moments when they feel that the world is conspiring against them, when everything feels out of control and when their only remaining defence is to attack, viciously. 'Everything was getting on top of me! It was all going wrong!' Perhaps that's what happened with Vinnie on the night of the disco.

In the television series *The Sopranos*, there's a recurring motif. Tony Soprano is a man whose every moment is spent controlling other people. The effort and anxiety of this is exhausting. But as the child of an unreliable mother, his overwhelming need has been to avoid dependency, and so he does this by controlling and, where necessary, killing other people. He becomes head of an alternative (Mafia) family which functions as an extension of himself. This family he *can* control – unlike his wife and children who, quite rightly, refuse to be controlled.

More than once, a family of ducks alights on the water of Tony's swimming pool. Spellbound, he watches and, rather than shoot them, is moved, glimpsing a family coming and going as it pleases, a world of relationships beyond the exhausting tyranny of narcissistic control. The ducks don't stay long. As soon as the babies have grown, they fly off, perhaps reminding Tony of his inability to escape the world he's created.

He takes all this to his therapist and tries to talk about it. But because he's working hard to control his therapist in the same subtle and not-so-subtle ways he works to control all relationships, he feels no better.

I think Vinnie briefly became Tony Soprano, and I was probably lucky not to be head-butted. Kernberg (1992) writes that 'The primary aim of one consumed by hatred is to destroy its object, a specific object of unconscious fantasy, and this object's conscious derivatives…' (p.23). What he means is that hatred is an attempt to destroy what we experience – rightly or wrongly – as 'bad' mothering. For fifteen seconds, I became all the unfairness, unkindness and neglect in Vinnie's life – I was responsible for it all. Kernberg goes on, 'the object is at bottom both needed and desired, and its destruction is equally needed and desired…' (p.23). In other words, Vinnie needed me because I represented the possibility of fairness, kindness and care ('good' mothering) but, because needing those things made him dependent and vulnerable, he hated me for causing the need and hated those needy parts of himself – in Symington's (1993) phrase – 'attempting to come to birth' (p.86). Kernberg goes on to argue that a therapist's attempts to stand up to a client's hatred may actually be experienced by the client as an attack. Certainly, whenever anyone stands up to Tony Soprano, their days are immediately numbered, and the fact that I didn't back away from my confrontation with Vinnie by the tennis courts probably did put me in danger.

I sat in his living room, trying to understand, trying to negotiate a way through our conversation so that his relationship with me and the Youth Centre didn't have to end. As I've said, running away would have been easy for him. Kernberg (1992) writes:

> Primitive hatred also takes the form of an effort to destroy the potential for a gratifying human relationship and for learning something of value in that interaction. Underlying this need to destroy reality and communication in intimate relationships is, I believe, unconscious and conscious envy of the object, particularly of an object not dominated from within by similar hatred. (p.25)

HATRED AND ENVY

One of the functions of narcissistic control (evinced by Tony Soprano and briefly by Vinnie) is to eliminate envy. *If I can control you and make you part of me, then I have no reason to envy you because I possess and control everything that you represent.* Because young people are uncertain and unconfident about themselves, they're necessarily envious of each other: envy expressed in constant day-to-day comparisons with each other and expressed powerfully in relation to boyfriends and girlfriends. Young people are forever worried that a plot is afoot and that their lover is about to be stolen by an envious rival, unconsciously recalling the way in which their mothers were once stolen from them.

When this kind of break-up does happen, all hell breaks loose. Everyone's nerves are raw and, after the break-up, there are strict unwritten rules about how much time should respectfully elapse before new suitors are allowed to reveal themselves. Presumably, these strict rules exist because envy is such a powerful and primitive force. Klein (1957) suggests that we envy our mothers because we believe that they have what we need but, for some reason, won't let us have it. Freud's (1900) Oedipus theory is mocked when it's interpreted literally to mean that boys *actually* want to have sex with their mothers. It's a much more interesting theory when understood metaphorically as an attempt to describe an unconscious wish to possess our parents' love in an original, undifferentiated relationship.

I'm sure that part of Vinnie envied my seeming ability to get along with all sorts of people and my imagined ability to fuck the Youth Centre whenever I wanted. It could be argued that boys call each other 'motherfucker' and, at the height of arguments, tell each other to 'Go fuck your mother!' because of their own unconscious, envious desire to possess their mothers, to have their mothers to themselves, sharing them with nobody and becoming the object of their mothers' total, full-time love. Regardless of whether the lost lover is a metaphorical mother or an actual boyfriend or girlfriend, hatred becomes a way of dealing with our envy of (what we imagine to be) the other person's new opportunities and admirers, independence, self-reliance, confidence, friends. *She doesn't need me any more!*

'I fucking hate her!'

'Because…?'

'Because she's so *up herself*! She thinks she's *it*! She tries to get everyone on her side and she thinks the sun shines out of her arse!'

It's hard to help young people think about envy because its roots are so primitive and because they're ashamed of it. Having been threatened by Vinnie, towering over me and behaving as if I was entirely worthless, it was tempting to believe that he really didn't need me. I think the opposite was true and that was precisely why he behaved as he did. Describing just such a loving-and-hating 'schizoid' person, Fairbairn (1952) writes, 'since the joy of loving seems hopelessly barred to him, he may as well deliver himself over to the joy of hating and obtain what satisfaction he can out of that' (p.27). There are young people who seem happier with the simple certainty of hatred, because to love and hate someone is too difficult. They defend themselves against such a painful paradox by keeping love and hate separate, splitting them apart. Kernberg (1992) writes:

> Hatred exists in a dialectic relation with love. Hatred implies an intense involvement with an object of past or potential love, an object that at some time was deeply needed. Hatred is, first of all, hatred of the frustrating object, but at the same time it is also hatred of the loved and needed object from whom love was expected and from whom frustration is unavoidable. In its origins, hatred is the consequence of the incapacity to eliminate frustration through rage, and it goes beyond rage in a lasting need to eliminate the object. (p.213)

This is the narcissistic illusion: *I can kill off my need by killing off the object of my need.* Some people become more and more grandiose (like Vinnie, rising up in front of me) as they try harder and harder to control everyone and everything. Every rebuff is experienced as a personal attack on themselves, an attack which is frightening and hateful. But it's those slippery relationships that are to blame. As Symington (1993) writes, 'the core of narcissism is a hatred of the relational' (p.18). What could be simpler, then, than to withdraw from relationships altogether rather than risk what would genuinely feel like being destroyed, annihilated. Surrendering to a give-and-take relationship would feel like losing all control, all that hard-won sense of self. So hatred becomes a last, desperate defence. 'We try to control annihilation anxiety by controlling objects we imagine responsible for it,' writes Eigen (2006, p.48).

Vinnie attacked what he most wanted. Alford (2006) writes that the extent to which a mother 'is able to contain the child's hatred and envy, will make an enormous difference in how well the child is able to integrate its experiences of loving and hating' (p.222). My job as a mother-figure was to withstand his attack and not retaliate.

But trapped in the darkness, trapped in Vinnie's glare, the difference between relaxed, active containment and frightened, passive inertia was subtle.

I remember Maddie who began our first counselling session by telling me what a wonderful counsellor I was reported to be. She was very articulate – old for her sixteen years and obviously keen to establish an adult relationship with me. I found myself immediately enjoying our knowing jokes and asides. I was flattered. There were certainly difficult circumstances in her life, but she was happy to talk about these and seemed well able to understand whatever insights I offered. She was always on time and seemed keen to continue our meetings.

However, I started to be uncomfortably aware that I was supposed to be a wonderful counsellor yet knew almost nothing about her father. I asked about him but was assured that there was nothing to tell; he was no longer part of her life and she'd stopped even thinking about him. He really wasn't an issue, she said, smiling back at her wonderful counsellor.

We continued meeting.

And then, several weeks later, she didn't come and didn't send a message. She also missed our next meeting with no explanation. This wasn't the behaviour of the reliable adult she'd purported to be. She didn't reply to my enquiring letter and I didn't see her for the best part of a year.

I was left feeling rubbished to the extent that I'd originally been worshipped. I told myself that she was getting me to feel *her* anger, *her* experience of being discarded by her father. This may have been true but I think there was more to it. After all, she managed to avoid me for a whole year and, even in a school spread over a big campus, that's an achievement. It meant that, unbeknown to me, she always saw me coming and always found a way of avoiding me.

I think this was more than just Maddie giving me a dose of the anger and uselessness she probably felt herself. In terms of what I've been describing, I think she spent a year hating me – hating me because I'd represented her hope for a relationship freed from the need to control me. Symington (1993) writes, 'When hope gleams, the narcissistic currents inside do all in their power to pull down this new-found figure' (p.87). I'd failed her because, while we were meeting, she'd continued to control the relationship. Despite my probing, she'd remained in charge of whatever we talked about and, now that we were no longer meeting, she still controlled the relationship, avoiding me with complete success.

We never addressed her underlying envy of me. Klein (1957) writes that 'Excessive idealisation... becomes also an important defence against envy, because if the object is exalted so much that comparison with it becomes impossible, envy is counteracted' (p.217). I think Maddie envied what she imagined to be my 'wonderful' power as a counsellor to understand and enter into relationships without being discarded or destroyed. But, at the same time, she hated that power and wanted to spoil it. It was the power of her father to leave her and to make new relationships elsewhere. I think her best version of a relationship was the collusive, uneasily adult one we established whereby she remained in control and we never talked about her father. So I wasn't actually respecting her defences, letting her go at her own pace or any of the other things I'd told myself at the time. I was simply colluding and, because she stayed in control of yet another relationship, I failed her. I think I was right not to challenge Vinnie as he glared at me in the dark. I was right to stand my ground, saying nothing, waiting and hoping for the moment to pass. But with Maddie, I should have drawn her attention to what I sensed was happening between us without blaming or criticising her but merely offering the observation as a way of describing something important. If I'd managed to do that without making her feel ashamed, we might have been able to try a more give-and-take relationship.

HATRED RECIPROCATED

Feeling frustrated and rubbished, it's easy to be angry with young people like Maddie and easy to envy *them*. Unlike adults, they can still get away with so much and they have so much going for them – their health, their youth, their energy – so many opportunities. It's easy for adults to respond to young people's hatred by hating them back. However calm and warm-hearted I may have seemed to Vinnie as I sat in his living room, part of me was still furious with him; part of me wanted to take revenge and ban him from ever coming to the Youth Centre again. I felt like saying, 'How dare you threaten me the other night! After all I've done for you! Helping you with all your bloody family problems! How dare you!'

I've spent a lot of time working with teachers for whom the thought that they might necessarily hate their students is quite out of the question. 'Of course not!' they say. 'We care passionately about all our students, otherwise we wouldn't be doing this difficult job. How ridiculous! If we hated students we wouldn't go out of our way to support them. We wouldn't be so hard-working, so patient, so dedicated!'

For several years I worked with a teacher who was all of these things – hard-working, patient, dedicated – supporting countless young people as they went through countless crises. And then, one summer, he got an unspecified illness with strange rashes, a persistently low mood and complete loss of energy. He found himself crying a lot and unable to get out of bed in the morning. His doctor diagnosed depression, and it was several months before I saw him again, back at work but still looking tired and drawn.

He talked of feeling guilty about all the young people he'd let down. 'You know how much they mean to me,' he said, 'and I've been working with them for over twenty years!'

I said that I didn't doubt his great dedication and compassion. 'These things are absolutely true, and I wonder whether there might also be a small part of you which hates them?'

He looked puzzled.

'Why not? Think about it! Their perpetual inability to know what's good for them, their constant fights, their drugs, their pregnancies, their laziness, their rudeness…'

He laughed out loud. 'It feels like that sometimes!'

Something seemed to shift and, as we talked, he seemed to recover some energy, to feel lighter, relieved.

As I've been describing, it's a basic tenet of psychoanalytic theory (Klein 1957) that a baby loves *and* hates its mother – loving her when she provides and hating her when she doesn't. For her part, the mother absorbs these feelings and feels similarly ambivalent about the baby who is the most wonderful thing imaginable as well as being the most spiteful and destructive. But it's very difficult for a mother to admit to feeling anything other than undying love for her baby, screaming in the next room. Mothers are expected to be saintly and selfless, and any woman who doesn't live up to this is apparently beyond our comprehension.

Teachers are in a similar position. They're *in loco parentis*, expected to care about all their students, to look after them, to move heaven and earth to support them. But part of what teachers get back from their students is – inevitably – hatred. Hatred for all the teachers' imperfections and shortcomings, for all the things that go wrong and aren't right with the world. Teachers absorb this stuff, week after week after week. But there are lots of things about the job that we enjoy, they say. So who could possibly admit to feelings of hatred as well as kindness and compassion towards students? I think young people hate and are also hated. Savage (2007) describes the way young people have been resented by adults for centuries and across continents. Because young people represent so much, they receive so much of the projected hatred of adults. All those opportunities! All that youth and energy! And all that ingratitude and time-wasting! Young people internalise the hatred of adults and feel it. It's impossible to separate their expressed hatred of adults from adults' usually unexpressed, covert hatred of young people. Mother and baby, parent and child are affected by each other.

It's tempting to believe that there are some people who hate and others who don't; that murderers, for example, are somehow different from other people, possessed of a capacity to hate which ordinary citizens don't share. I think that we all have the capacity to hate and that people who murder are merely (and usually only temporarily) at one extreme end of the continuum. I think that hatred exists and is normal in anyone who takes seriously the job of teaching or nursing or youth work or counselling or working with young offenders or social work or any other job with young people. The problem is what to do about it, because the hatred won't go away. It can be denied, of course, but the danger is that, as with my long-suffering teacher, the effort of containing it over the years is eventually too much and it emerges as depression.

It can be projected on to young people through the ways in which we wind them up, getting them to express our hatred for us. (We can then exclude them from school for behaving in hateful ways.) It can leak out in jokes and asides. It can be displaced into relationships with colleagues, partners and families, who become the unwitting targets of our pent-up feelings.

Winnicott (1947/1958) writes about a psychiatrist (in the days when psychiatrists were assumed to be male), 'However much he loves his patients he cannot avoid hating them and fearing them, and the better he knows this the less will hate and fear be the motives determining what he does to his patients' (p.195). Acknowledging our adult hatred seems the most useful starting point. *Like any committed professional, I care passionately about young people. Part of me therefore hates them.*

'So discos are boring because everyone's busy getting off with everyone else?'

Vinnie nodded. 'Discos are really boring. They're all right when you're a kid but, at my age, you want to be going out with your mates.'

I remembered that his 'mates' on the night in question were two much younger boys. But they were presumably better than nothing – transitional friendships, easing his separation from the Youth Centre. 'You've contributed a lot to the Youth Centre and you've been coming a long time, Vinnie.'

'Too long.'

I wondered what he meant. Too long to be needing support from a Youth Centre family? Too long to be needing affection? Too long to be living with such an embarrassing need? Better to get rid of it, maybe. Get rid of it once and for all. Smash its face. Its stupid, fucking face.

'Can you say more about the other night, Vinnie?'

'Not really…'

'More about what you were feeling?'

'No! I was pissed off!'

There was no point in pushing him. If hatred comes from somewhere primitive before words, then 'pissed off' was probably as close as he could get.

'Have you heard anything from your mum?'

The television was still on with Tom and Jerry chasing each other around, smashing each other over the head and coming back for more.

'No! She knows about my step-mum but she's not bothered. She sent me some money at Christmas and that was the last I heard from her. Anyway, why are you asking? You know I don't like talking about it!'

I did know that Vinnie's mother had walked out on him and his father three years earlier and that Vinnie always avoided talking about it. Bowlby (1973) describes hatred as 'elicited in children and adolescents who not only experience repeated separations but are constantly subjected to the threat of being abandoned' (p.288). I wondered how much Vinnie was now provoking the Youth Centre to abandon him by banning him so that, getting older, he didn't have to feel that he was abandoning the Youth Centre. Perhaps hatred condensed all those ambivalent feelings into one simplified scream.

'I know you don't like talking about your mum, Vinnie. I was just thinking that it must be difficult sometimes, living with your dad and step-mum...?'

It would have been easier for Vinnie to talk if he'd been going out with someone. Then he'd have had someone to receive his love and assuage the bad, persecuting, hurtful feelings. In crude psychological terms, his first girlfriend had deserted him and not yet been replaced. The wound was still raw. Mollon (2001) describes the way certain relationships ('selfobjects') serve to regulate our feelings in the absence of any internalised capacity to do this for ourselves. As boys often say about their girlfriends, 'She calms me down.'

Vinnie shrugged. 'Living with my dad and that bitch doesn't really bother me because I'm not at home that often.'

A little is often a lot with young people. It's important not to push too hard in case the defensive shutters go up completely. All I could do – as tactfully as possible – was to give Vinnie opportunities to tell his feelings so that he didn't have to enact them at someone else's expense. I could have asked more about his mother, which was where the hurt, betrayal and hatred would have been most acute, or I could have asked more about his father and step-mother, which might have been easier for him to talk about. I certainly wasn't going to ask about what the Youth Centre meant to him or anything fancy like that, because to Vinnie – consciously – the Youth Centre was no more than a youth centre, for God's sake. It wasn't some kind of mother!

I tried once more. 'A lot's changed for you over the years...'

'You could say that!'

'All the stuff with your mum, with leaving school, with your dad getting together with your step-mum, with you and your mates...'

He nodded.

'Good in some ways?'

He nodded again.

'Bad in others?'

He took a breath, a big one. And breathed out again. Slowly.

I said nothing. A long, slow sigh was Vinnie talking.

We still had some unfinished business. 'I know you've got other things going on in your life, but I hope you'll keep in touch with the Youth Centre,' I said. 'What are we going to do about the other night?'

'I think you should ban me.'

'What? Completely? I don't want to do that.'

'Well, for a bit.'

'For how long?'

'A month?'

We agreed on it. Tom and Jerry were still chasing each other with unending, violent affection.

He never came back to the Youth Centre. Not conspicuously. Not resentfully or swearing at me in the street. He just didn't come back and I didn't worry. His capacity to hate hadn't changed any more (I hope) than his capacity to love: those are givens. What may have been affected slightly was his capacity to *tolerate* a residual, unconscious hatred of mothers, step-mothers, girlfriends, boyfriends and youth workers – people you can't help needing in your life but about whom you can't help having mixed feelings.

4

Making Up

So far, this book has been about the complexities of boy-friend and girlfriend relationships; in particular, the way young people's love and hatred of their parents affects those relationships – sometimes directly, sometimes indirectly, but always in some way. This chapter is about the ways in which a counsellor or other professional might help a young person with these complexities by offering a relationship with a par-ent-*figure*, the experience of which will have subtle effects on a young person's thinking about boyfriends and girlfriends.

As I've described, our earliest relationship is with a mother or mothering-figure and we take that relationship into subsequent relationships, continuing to work at the many unconscious conflicts we've internalised along the way. In particular, we work at resolving the old conflict between love and hate, the awful paradox whereby we find ourselves capable of loving and hating the same person. All other emo-tions come from this, argues Nussbaum (2001). So until we find a way of living with the paradox, we continue to divide other people into those we love and those we hate, because to have mixed feelings about anyone seems impossible.

But things develop. It's a developmental achievement (Winnicott 1965) when we can tolerate our love and hatred, our hope and disappointment simultaneously; when we realise that the object of our strong feelings may not be perfect but that really doesn't matter because, as a mothering-figure, she's good enough. She's a mixture. Like us.

Arriving at this realisation may take years, and inevitably there are times along the way when we fear and hate her. We hate her because it seems that she won't let us have what we long for – her full-time, adoring, perfect love (Klein 1935/1975). But, in hating her, our intention is never to destroy her because we'd also be destroying the object of our longing. Alford (2006) writes that 'Our deepest fear, as we grow older, is that we shall confuse love and hate, and so destroy all we love and care about' (p.221). Having hated so vehemently, our dawning realisation as we get older is that we may have injured or destroyed the object of our hatred. So, once we're able to bear our own ambivalence, we look to make up for the past.

It comes as a relief to find that the object of our hatred is, in fact, still alive and flourishing. Somehow that hatred was borne by a robust and sensible mothering-figure who didn't take it personally but understood it as a necessary part of our growing up, a developmental response to envy and frustration, to the imperfection of the world. Guiltily, and before it's too late, we set about 'making reparation' (Klein 1929/1975), ensuring that the object of our hatred is unhurt and anxiously giving back to her some of the love she's given to us. Winnicott (1965) describes the guilty child developing a 'capacity for concern', starting to take personal responsibility, repairing damaged relationships and beginning to treasure the person he or she once hated. Winnicott (1958) writes that 'The attainment of a capacity for making reparation in respect of personal guilt is one of the most important steps in the development of the healthy human being' (p.91).

Whether this once-hated person happens to be a mother or father, girlfriend or boyfriend, young people call the process 'making up'. 'I'm thinking of making up with her… He

wants to make up with me... We've agreed to make up...'
The love and hatred originally focused on a mothering-figure
doesn't necessarily go away but is played out in relationships
with friends and enemies, boyfriends and girlfriends...

And counsellors. My job is to help a young person move
on from a view of the world where things are either good
or bad, loveable or hateful, towards an ability to tolerate
mixed feelings. Once that process has begun, I support the
young person's attempts to make up for whatever may have
happened in the past and to feel less guilty about his or her
original hatred. This is important, because without the opportunities or the confidence to make up, young people can
be left with a sense that they're destructive, bad people who
might as well spend the rest of their lives being destructive
and bad. Winnicott (1965) is right: 'Failure of reparation
leads to a losing of the capacity for concern, and its replace-
ment by primitive forms of guilt and anxiety' (p.82).

Sometimes making up is easy. Sometimes there are mothers or mothering-figures only too happy to sit down and talk
about what's happened, forgiving without bitterness or re-
crimination. But sometimes there aren't, and, in any case,
some young people don't trust their ability to make amends.
As Gomez (1997) writes:

> These people feel that their anger is too overwhelming
> or destructive for repair to be possible; they may have
> lost sight of, or never really gained, belief in their own
> goodness as the basis for reparation; or their guilt may
> itself feel too persecutory and attacking. (p.43)

Without opportunities to make up with an available,
actual mothering-figure, young people are obliged to look
elsewhere.

Some look to school. I've written about 'school' as an *unconscious* mothering-figure for young people who love school
and hate school (Luxmoore 2008). Many who ostentatiously

hated school when they were younger are later delighted to be given opportunities by school to make amends. For example, they jump at the chance to take responsibility for younger students, rising to the challenge and amazing those long-suffering teachers with whom they once fought. They organise fundraising events for charity; they help on residential trips; they sometimes report bullying; they sometimes break up fights and then, having made up with school, they leave, looking back fondly where, a year earlier, they'd have sworn that school was the worst thing ever to have happened to them while feeling – privately – that they were probably the worst thing ever to have happened to school.

Winnicott (1965) argues that the mothering-figure must provide opportunities for reparation if the child is ever to move beyond its guilt for having hated so powerfully. But staff in schools are understandably reluctant to provide reparative opportunities: 'Why should we trust him after all the things he's done? He's the last person we should be trusting!'

I didn't know Rosie at all, but when her name was put forward for a scheme I was running it was met with disbelief by certain teachers. I was planning to work with students who'd been troublemakers themselves. I would train and supervise them to work with younger students who were beginning their own troublemaking years. Rosie's teachers protested that she was far too disruptive to be trusted. She'd be a bad influence and, besides, she was still badly behaved in lessons. The other names on my list were worth a go, they said. It was just Rosie!

All the students were keen to be involved and eventually did their work well. Rosie was interesting. She was late for all our training sessions but, having arrived, got stuck into the role-playing with relish, playing disruptive students with predictable ease but proving equally adept at being herself in a supportive role, listening to these imaginary disruptive students. She learned not to give them advice but to listen instead for their feelings and for underlying family dynamics.

Because of her absences from school and my subsequent difficulties in catching up with her, she eventually worked with only one student. They had two meetings.

She and I met to talk about how the meetings had gone.

'It was easy,' Rosie said. 'Not a problem! I told her what it was like for me when I was her age and I told her not to get into trouble because it's not worth it!'

So much for not giving advice! So much for my delicate counselling skills! Rosie saw no reason to discuss it further.

I bumped into the younger student in the corridor and asked her how the meetings with Rosie had gone.

'Fine,' said the girl.

'Useful?'

'Yeah!'

A year after Rosie had left school, I walked past a figure sitting on the school wall one evening. I smiled but had no idea who it was.

Then it dawned on me.

'You didn't recognise me, did you!'

I admitted that I hadn't. 'How are you?'

'All right,' she said. 'I'm at college now.'

I said I was pleased. 'I don't suppose you're doing anything like the stuff we did with the younger students last year?'

'Haven't got time,' she said. 'Too much coursework!'

I asked what she was studying.

Rosie's reply made absolute sense. 'Child and social care!'

I never found out about her life away from school or the reasons for her behaviour in school. I imagine that she fought with her teachers at school as the continuation of a fight she was having with her parents at home. I imagine that she began life loving, then found herself hating everything, then taking her feelings out on school and then feeling bad about herself.

Teachers are good at making sure that young people know when they've been bad. Sometimes they're less good at making sure that a young person's sense of badness isn't reinforced. Rosie got one brief reparative opportunity before she left school. Other young people leave school still unconsciously looking for opportunities to make up. Some find jobs where they can lavish on children or animals the love they never had opportunities to express before. Suzanne, who bullied her way through the first three years of school, tells me that she wants to be a nurse. Marcus, who hated asking for help, wants to be a psychologist. Donny wants to be a plumber, understanding and fitting things together where once he tore everything apart. Mimi hated her parents, left home at fourteen, started using heroin at fifteen and is now living in a hostel. Whenever I see her around town, she's accompanied by two dogs – not snarling, muscular bodyguards but scruffy little things she rescued from friends who weren't looking after them properly, she says.

In their own ways, these young people are unconsciously making up for having hated so much and are reconnecting with their capacity to love. For many, the ups and downs of these processes are focused on boyfriends or girlfriends. Vikram comes to see me, wanting to talk about his girlfriend. 'We broke up last week but I think it might have been a mistake,' he says. 'I miss her already. We've been going out for ages and she's the only person I can really talk to. But she reckons we don't spend enough time together and she reckons the relationship isn't going anywhere, which is news to me. The only problem I can see was that there's this other girl I fancied a bit and I made the mistake of mentioning it to Kate last week and she went ballistic! So I suppose it was my fault really. But, to be honest, I don't know what I feel any more. I know I'll always have feelings for Kate. My mum really likes her and we'd even talked about getting engaged.' He twists uncomfortably in his chair. 'I just don't know what to do…'

He's stuck. Winnicott (1971) writes that 'Psychotherapy has to do with two people playing together' (p.38). In that sense, Vikram and I have to start playing, finding ways of getting unstuck, picking up his feelings like toys and passing them between us – examining them, turning them over, looking at them from different angles, seeing what they can do, how far they can stretch, how much pressure they can bear.

Playing is also a kind of practising for life (see Chapter 2). And the situation with his girlfriend is an opportunity for Vikram to practise because there'll be plenty of other occasions in his life when he'll be torn between opposite feelings. 'Should I stay or should I go? What are the pros and cons? Do I love her or not love her?' Behind his dumbfounded, hurt, indignant words, there'll be other meanings with which to play. When Vikram says, 'She's the only person I can really talk to' he might mean, *Kate always agrees with me.* He might mean *I've always been able to get my own way with Kate* or *Unlike other people, Kate's prepared to listen to me going on and on.* 'She's the only person I can really talk to' might even mean *Kate lets me have sex with her whenever I want!* When he says, 'She reckons we don't spend enough time together and she reckons the relationship isn't really going anywhere' he might mean *I know perfectly well that we never spend any time together and I know the relationship isn't going anywhere but, because that's my fault and I don't want to take the blame, I'll try to make myself seem like the innocent party.* In my experience with young people, 'There's this other girl I fancied a bit' usually means *There's this other girl I fancied a lot and still do fancy a lot.* 'Mentioning it to Kate' can mean *I tested the water with Kate to see whether she'd mind if I had sex with the other girl but Kate wasn't prepared to be treated like that and made me choose between them*. His lament, 'I'll always have feelings for Kate' might mean *I don't love Kate any more but I don't want to be portrayed as the bad guy*. 'My mum really likes her' could mean *My mum really likes her and so I've gone off Kate* or it could mean *My mum really likes Kate and so I'd better keep going out with Kate to please my mum*. It could mean *My mum really likes Kate and that was the reason why I went out with Kate in the first place*. 'We'd even talked about getting engaged' is what some young people say to make their love sound real and to make themselves sound like grown-ups. Even Vikram's 'I just don't know what to do' may not be straightforward. It might mean *I have genuinely mixed feelings*, but it could also mean *I know exactly what to do but I'm afraid to do it!*

Young people usually bring a stuckness to counselling, a fixed view of the world. To play with that stuckness is to loosen it, to find new meanings and young people are understandably resistant to this. If I were to offer Vikram my rather cynical decoding of his words, he'd storm out of the room – humiliated and furious. My decoding might be accurate but, for him, its timing would be insensitive and its cynical tone humiliating. He'd never trust me again.

So we have to play together without anyone being humiliated. I ask and he tells me his first memories of Kate; how they started going out together after a party at a friend's house. At various points in the story, I ask how he felt and, whenever his reply sounds simplistic, we play with it.

'I fancied her, the moment I saw her!'

'For her body or for her personality?'

'Both, of course!'

'Because she was fun?'

'Yeah!'

'And intelligent?'

'She's really brainy. She gets really good grades.'

'What was it like when you first met, Vikram?'

'I don't know,' he says. 'I was too pissed at the time!'

'When you were sober?'

'She was good to talk to, yeah. She's good at listening.'

'To you?'

'I suppose so.' At this point, he gets worried, checking the rules of our game. 'Why are you asking?'

'Because it's important to understand how we feel and because the way we feel is usually complicated.'

'You can say that again! Like I said, I don't know what I feel about her.'

'Because of feeling mixed?'

'Yeah!'

'Fancying her and... What else? Fancying her and finding her boring? Fancying her and resenting her?'

'Why would I resent her?'

'Because she's a strong person? Because she's got her own friends? I don't know...'

'I don't resent her,' he says, 'but I don't like it when she talks about me behind my back. She says she doesn't but I know she does and then I can't trust her, can I?'

And so we go on — trying out ideas, exploring possibilities, wondering whether some of his feelings might be more mixed than he'd allowed. Our conversation becomes a play area where Vikram can look at himself from different angles, where his thinking can evolve and change, no longer so simplistic, no longer so stuck.

Boyfriends and girlfriends allow young people to practise amorous, intimate, sometimes sexual relationships and, importantly, to practise not knowing exactly what they feel about those relationships (see Chapter 2). Not knowing softens the old loving-or-hating certainties. Counselling is a chance to practise not knowing about yet another relationship.

Writing about therapeutic groups, Garland (1982) describes someone coming to a group, expecting advice and solutions to a preoccupying problem. However, that problem is quickly overshadowed by the experience of being in the group. Because this experience is so strange and different, it allows the person to feel differently and this shifts things *internally* for the person. The preoccupying, external problem no longer looks the way it did. Something has changed.

I think this process happens in counselling. A young person like Vikram comes to me with an urgent, sometimes burning problem. We talk about it but we talk about other, related things as well. We talk about the past and the future. We enter into a relationship with each other, a relationship with its own satisfactions and dissatisfactions. The young person who comes in full of angry, unfair stories gets a chance to talk about his dreams. The shy person gets a chance to be vociferous and indignant. In short, the relationship in the counselling room allows a young person to play, to practise being different, to bear not knowing. Perhaps counselling is about failing to solve the problem but understanding ourselves and the problem better so that it no longer seems so problematic. Weeks later, we still sometimes find ourselves talking about the original problem, but things have moved on. Events have happened outside our counselling sessions. New problems have emerged along with new perspectives.

There's method in this. We don't simply sit around chatting about football or whatever we happened to be watching on television last night – significant as those things sometimes are. We deliberately talk about the most important things in a young person's life (families, friends, feelings), but it's the young person's continuing experience of our own relationship which allows these seemingly mysterious internal shifts to happen.

The original problem is usually the externalisation of an internal problem. Something internal has to shift, therefore, before the external problem can be affected. That shift happens in the interplay between two people. Fourteen-year-old

Cheryl comes with an external problem – a big one. She's been urgently referred to me because, not only has she involved herself in unsavoury internet relationships, trading sexual stories with older men, but she's also met one of these men and, after the briefest of courtships, allowed him to have sex with her. Lots of professionals are now involved and Cheryl knows that they disapprove.

The trouble is that she can't see it. 'It was my choice,' she insists. 'He didn't force me to do anything. I wanted to!'

I'm tempted to add my own outrage to that of the professionals. But they've done their job – mine is to listen to Cheryl's big, external problem and make a relationship with her because – of course – there's more. There's a whole fourteen-year-old life to disentangle and think about.

I learn that, like other young people who seem to be in a state of perpetual agitation (checking their phones, smoking, checking their phones, shouting…), she externalises everything. Every time we meet she's dressed as a different person – hippy chick one minute, Hell's Angel the next; glamour model one week, street hooligan the next. The many parts of her self (Luxmoore 2008) are displayed for the world to see – Cheryl the child, the thug, the whore, the pugilist… She has no sense of privacy, telling me her uncensored thoughts and feelings as they occur – all her fantasies and nightmares, her childhood and sexual experiences, the boys she's fancied and the men she's had sex with. It's as if her inner world gets tipped out on to my carpet once a week, leaving nothing inside. *Look, that's everything! Nothing left!*

This might be exciting for a counsellor believing that 'honesty' and the expression of strong feelings are ends in themselves. But they aren't. What Cheryl does is dangerous because it leaves her with no internal life, no sense of existing unless she's actively, *externally* in contact with other people. She'll have learned to tip everything out because, in the past, keeping her feelings to herself will have been too difficult. She's never learned to wait, trusting that someone will eventually notice her, because in the past, presumably, no one did. Instead, she's learned that you get noticed by behaving extravagantly. She's learned to express everything and keep nothing back so that now, when she seems to be sharing herself so wholeheartedly, so uninhibitedly, she's merely evacuating herself, defending herself against feeling anything inside. Whenever a feeling emerges within her, Cheryl immediately expels it as words or as some kind of behaviour.

She loves and she hates. When she loves, she expresses her love with over-the-top gestures: a new friend is immediately a best friend, perfect in every way; an interesting man is immediately a lover to be trusted absolutely. She spends hours on the phone to these people. She gives them ridiculously expensive presents. And when Cheryl hates, she fights with fists or sends obscene messages. She tells the world all about whoever she's hating at the moment and about what she's going to do to that person. 'It's just the way I am!' she says. 'I've always been that way! If people don't like it, then that's their problem!' It's as if she can't be by herself, feeling her own feelings. She's desperate for loving relationships but can't begin to internalise them.

Except, possibly, in counselling. When she was growing up, she says, her mother was always out, working in pubs or off with boyfriends. I sense that one of the things Cheryl has never experienced is what it's like to be in close proximity with another person without having to be touching that person or speaking to that person to know that he or she is still there and still paying attention. She gets that experience in counselling. She doesn't need to panic because I'm not about to leave her and go off to the pub. We can practise going slowly. We can leave silences. When she behaves or speaks extravagantly, I don't have to react extravagantly but can listen and think. We talk quietly. When she tells me about extreme behaviour (swearing at people, cutting herself, getting drunk), I ask about what she was feeling at the time, trying to give her the experience of an internal emotional world being understandable to another person and shared with that person without needing external behaviour to get her point across.

We ban the word 'love' as too simplistic, too generalised. Whenever she mentions it, I ask her to be more precise. She recognises what I'm doing and laughs. Eventually she hears herself saying the word, and we smile without me needing to interrupt. We talk about gradations of love – different kinds of affection, different kinds of friendship, different feelings about parents, teachers, men.

As the weeks go by, she quietens. She seems less impulsive, even complaining that things are 'boring'. And I'm pleased because I think she's describing an *ordinariness* whereby life no longer needs to be extreme to be real. She can exist without crises or alarm. In our counselling relationship, I'm the mother-figure and she's my baby. I don't forget that she's there. I pay attention to her even when she isn't crying or screaming. I'm interested in her, enjoying her happiness and sympathising with her sadnesses. And when I'm not paying attention or not understanding properly, she doesn't have to panic but can wait, knowing that I'll be back soon and that my misunderstandings can be corrected.

Cheryl is developing what Fonagy *et al.* (2004) would call an 'internalised reflective self-function', an ability to think about and observe herself without which her loving and hating must forever be split and externalised. Potentially, counselling gives Cheryl an opportunity to feel ambivalent, to make up, to experience herself as capable of loving and being loved without having to *enact* anything. Counselling gives her an experience of ordinary, slow, gradual loving

kindness which will be fundamental to any fulfilling relationships she'll have with boyfriends or girlfriends in the future.

I want to describe what I mean by that ordinary loving
kindness... Underneath all our relationships is a formative
relationship with the external world, with the 'other'. As I described in Chapter 3, 'normal' narcissism ('I am everything!')
usually gives way to an ability to appreciate another person's
separate existence and an ability to relate to that 'other'
person, sharing power, giving and taking, enjoying rather
than resenting the other person's separateness. The manner
in which young people engage or don't engage with me in
counselling usually mirrors the way in which they've learned
to engage or not engage with the otherness of other people,
beginning with their parents. Becky engages instantly, seeming to trust me and wanting to tell me about everything. Zac
seems willing but is unsure whether I'm on his side or not.
Louise says a lot but doesn't come back for our second session while Nisha is inscrutable and wary but keeps coming
back. Sophie is really hard work – unable to initiate any conversation or say what she really feels.

All these attachment styles (Bowlby 1969, 1973, 1980)
will be learned from young people's earlier experiences in
life and will be taken forward into boyfriend and girlfriend
relationships. I might predict that Becky will engage confidently but risk getting hurt by boyfriends who can't return
her enthusiasm. Zac will be forever unsure about whether his
girlfriend loves him or not. Louise will have one-night stands,
the way she has a one-session stand with me. Inscrutable,
wary Nisha will become someone's long-suffering, patient
girlfriend, while monosyllabic Sophie will struggle to engage
with anyone as an equal... My predictions may be hopelessly
wrong but, where a young person's attachment style is en-
trenched, the chance of that style being reproduced in other
relationships is greater.

Officially, these young people come to counselling seeking 'help' or 'advice' or 'someone who'll listen'. Unofficially, they come seeking love in the same way that they seek love from their parents, their school, their friends. And love is what they get.

At the psychotherapy society to which I belong, an eminent speaker gave a talk entitled 'Is it always counter-transference? Love in the therapeutic relationship'. He spoke about his relationship with a client and the love he felt towards her, which wasn't sexual love, he said. It wasn't the erotic love which tortures therapists and occasionally leads them to misuse their power. Nor was it counter-transference love, he added. In other words, he wasn't merely caught up in the relationship and unconsciously responding to whatever his client felt towards him as her therapist. No, he said. This was neither of those things. This was his own love for his client, pure and simple.

We attacked him. How could this be so? He must be deluding himself. It *must* have been counter-transferential love, some claimed, because *all* feelings towards clients are counter-transferential. She must have provoked the feeling in him. And it *must* have been sexual, they went on, because all love is implicitly sexual.

I sat by, wanting to stick up for him but uncertain of my ground. It sounded as if he'd committed some dreadful therapist's sin by admitting to having feelings about his client which were his own. I wanted to say that I think I love my clients too. I don't usually love them sexually but, when I do sense something sexual in our relationship, I discuss it with my supervisor in order to understand and bear it so that – at the very least – I never act on it. And, of course, there are times when my feelings are counter-transferential.

But there are also times when they're not. And those are the times when I do my best work. They're the times when

I'm touched by a young person's plight, moved by their honesty and resilience, delighted by their refusal to be cowed, humbled by their generosity towards others. I love these qualities in the young people I work with and, when they sense this, I think it's an important therapeutic moment. It's the moment, for example, when Danny is talking about the night of his father's death without looking at me but needing me to ask more... It's the moment when I suggest to Magda that, underneath everything, she has a 'Bollocks!' voice and we laugh together... It's the moment when Steve's been talking about his step-dad and suddenly looks at me and says, 'I don't like the fact that he's taken my mum away from me'... It's the moment when Sarah's relationship with Suzannah is going really well at long last and I say that I'm pleased and Sarah blushes, not knowing what to say...

I'm arguing that love happens and – within the necessary constraints of a therapeutic relationship with all its power imbalances – is productive. Freud famously wrote to Jung in 1906 that psychoanalysis is in essence a cure through love (McGuire 1974). It's when I *can't* love a young person that I'm in trouble; when my capacity to understand and empathise is begrudging or when I feel no compassion. Then our relationship stays stuck. There are young people who habitually make themselves unlovable because love is so unfamiliar that the prospect of being loved by another person endangers their hard-won independence, making them vulnerable. Mann (2002) writes, 'Love can close down psychological distance between individuals and, therefore, can be experienced as a threat to a fragile sense of self' (p.35). There are other young people who behave in an unlovable way, and the danger is that I respond accordingly: that's counter-transference. With other young people, their behaviour is a test, as if to say, 'See how unlovable I can be? *Now* try loving me!' I find it hard to love young people when they're lying or withholding information and I can't help them. I find it harder to love young people who keep missing our meetings. I know that these behaviours are essentially defensive but the problem is when I can't see beyond the defence, when a young person just seems to be *like that*.

I'm not describing any saintly, morally superior ability to love other people. I'm describing agapaic love – love that is altruistic, admiring and, in fact, terribly ordinary (Lomas 1973). It's an ordinariness that young people find hard to quantify because it's different from the romantic myth where our eyes are supposed to meet across a crowded room and suddenly *we know!* Sparks fly! There's magic, passion! (Centuries ago, struck by Cupid, we'd have been physically sick.) Sometimes young people have that experience and it's great. Or sometimes it's like that at the start. But then it changes; it becomes more ordinary and, as I've described in Chapter 2, it's hard for young people to know what that means. In Jonathan Swift's poem 'The Lady's Dressing Room' (1732) Strephon enters his beloved Celia's dressing room while she's out. He goes behind the scenes, looking round, inspecting all the things that support this beautiful woman – the sweaty clothes, smelly towels, knotted hairbrushes and filthy washbasin. Becoming more and more disillusioned, Strephon finally discovers the lavatory:

> Thus finishing his grand survey,
> Disgusted Strephon stole away
> Repeating in his amorous fits,
> Oh! Celia, Celia, Celia shits!

Vikram comes back to see me. As a counsellor and parent-figure, I'm inevitably the focus of young people's love and hatred – idealised one minute and demonised the next. What happens, more often than not, is that I become the young person's 'good' parent to set against the 'bad' one at home. I let young people believe this for as long as what they're getting seems to be helpful – a sense that they *are* lovable, that they *are* interesting. But then I work on demystifying myself and we talk a lot about disappointment and ordinariness, about people and things we can't control, about the 'otherness' of other people, about the fact that (in young's people's terms) shit happens. If I were a textbook psychoanalyst, I might encourage my young client to reflect on his or her feelings towards me. I might name them. A young person might say that these feelings don't exist ('I don't really feel like that about you!') and I might insist that they do (because they do, *theoretically*). However, all this would only serve to embarrass my client: nothing would be gained. So, as a counsellor with young people, I don't do that. I keep my thoughts to myself and we talk about fathers and mothers, boyfriends and girlfriends.

Like many young people, Vikram is wrestling with the apparent ordinariness of his sometime girlfriend, Kate, whom he fancied, who 'listened' to him and to whom he contemplated engagement. In our last few sessions, he's barely mentioned her, talking instead about his parents and about how annoying they are.

This time, I ask about Kate.

'We're back together again,' he says, 'but I'm not sure if it'll last. I mean, I really like her… I'm just not sure.'

I ask what she feels about things.

'She wants to give it another go,' he says, not really answering the question.

I wonder to myself whether he has any idea what Kate really feels and whether he's ever bothered to find out. 'We may love our partners,' writes Bramley (2008), 'but we also *use* them, as they use us, to make ourselves feel better' (p.12). In our sessions, I sometimes feel taken for granted by Vikram, as if I'm expected to service him. I wonder whether Kate feels the same. I wonder whether his parents have patiently, selflessly doted on their son, afraid to ask for anything in return, and I wonder what to do about my feeling because the danger is that Vikram and I are merely re-enacting what happens in all his relationships. To do nothing will be to perpetuate and collude with this way of relating to other people. Yet I'm wary of making here-and-now interpretations with young people – commenting on our relationship – for fear that it'll be too much to bear, too exposing, too embarrassing.

I could say exactly what I'm thinking, 'I feel as if I'm expected to service you, Vikram, and I wonder whether other people feel the same when they're with you?' He wouldn't understand and, if I explained, I imagine he'd feel humiliated as if I was accusing him of selfishness. Whatever his attachment style may be (wary, staying in control, getting rather than giving), it'll be a learned rather than a chosen style and he'll have learned it for a reason. It may be that trusting other people to be equal partners in a relationship feels too unsafe for Vikram. It may be that no one's ever empathised sufficiently with him and so he's never learned to empathise with other people… Either way, I think of his behaviour as defensive, as a way of dealing with anxiety.

I decide to say something. 'Maybe it's hard for you to let other people in at the moment, Vikram?' I suggest. 'Maybe you keep people at arm's length because you don't want to get hurt?'

'What do you mean?' he asks. 'Do you mean with Kate?'

'Not just with Kate. Maybe it's hard to trust other people?'

'It *is!*'

'It's certainly hard to trust your mum and dad…'

He agrees.

'And it's probably hard to trust me…'

He says nothing, thinking. 'I do trust you,' he says, 'but you meet with loads of other people as well.'

'And I might talk about you behind your back?'

'Maybe.'

'Like you imagine Kate does?'

'Maybe.'

We pause.

'I think you're right to be cautious,' I say. 'I think it's important to go slowly when it comes to trusting other people. It might take years to know whether you can trust Kate or me or anyone else because sometimes people *will* let you down... Even people who love you!'

He thinks about this.

'Good people can be disappointing, Vikram.'

He says nothing.

'Kate will be disappointing sometimes. I'll be disappointing sometimes. And your parents...' I wait for him to react. This is a key moment. If he can tolerate this idea, we're in business. If not, then I've misjudged the moment and set our relationship back.

To my relief, he smiles. 'If you ask me, everyone's a fucking disappointment!'

We laugh and talk about real love being ordinary and slow and clumsy and cumulative. This idea is really difficult for young people. Often they break up relationships because the spark, the magic, the passion has changed and in its place is something ordinary. I think this experience of ordinariness is an unconscious re-experiencing of an original disillusionment with our mothers. Coming to terms with a boyfriend or girlfriend's ordinariness is part of the process of accepting the fact that other people – mothers *and* lovers – are a mixture of the satisfactory and unsatisfactory. Counselling offers young people a chance to feel differently, to make up, no longer split between old loving and hating polarities. It's a chance to be loved ordinarily, knowing that the loving counsellor is neither perfect nor pathetic.

5

Breaking Up

There are break-ups with boyfriends and girlfriends which are spectacular (brazen infidelities, blazing rows) and other break-ups which are damp squibs (a brief text message, days of glum avoidance). There are young people who break up with each other at the first sign of trouble, and others who stay in unhappy relationships for fear of ever breaking up. Because of their earlier experiences of separation (Bowlby 1973), many young people have clear expectations about what the ending of any relationship will be like. This chapter is about the ways in which young people can (and do) use the ending of a counselling relationship – unconsciously – to practise for other relationships, making endings with other people seem more or less possible, seem like signs of strength or weakness. In other words, ending a counselling relationship provides information about how other relationships might or might not end.

For counsellors and for other professionals closely involved in young people's lives, the endings of working relationships with young people can be perplexing because they're so unpredictable. As a counsellor, I've worried for years that my own endings are messy and that I Must Do Better. I've told myself that I'm an expert at beginnings – at putting young people at their ease, explaining things clearly, normalising the situation and judging precisely how directive to be with each person. I know I'm good at this because, despite the initial weirdness of agreeing to meet with a strange man called a counsellor, closing the door and sitting down to talk with him, young people invariably come back. But I worry that when it comes to endings, to winding down and saying goodbye after weeks, months and sometimes years of meeting, our focus seems to get lost.

It's our last session.
Is it? Really? Oh my God, I didn't realise!

Maybe I get too tired. Maybe I'm secretly cross with young people for always growing up and leaving me, year after year after year. Maybe I'm technically or theoretically deficient in some important way when it comes to endings.

It's our last session.
Yeah, I know. Hey, you'll never guess what happened this week!

Where I work, the counselling service is integrated into the life of the school and I have a repertoire of involvements beyond individual counselling with students and staff. These involvements support the institution as a whole because the experience of being part of a good school is at least as therapeutic for young people as individual counselling. I come across young people in many contexts, therefore: the same student I saw for counselling behind closed doors in the morning I may later greet in the car park at lunchtime and sit with in a meeting after school about tackling homophobia. My boundaries are clear so that my relationships can be flexible. I learn names and say hello to as many people around school as possible. Purist psychodynamic practice may be useful for some adults but it's too weird for most young people: the model has to be adapted. And I adapt it a lot (I don't interpret the transference, I don't prolong the silences, I sometimes share my own experience) but still I worry about my endings.

It's our last session.
Oh, I thought we had one more?

I've tried counting the sessions down portentously to a Last One, listening for panic so that we can bear the panic together; listening for a revival of the original symptoms ('I've started to feel bad again') so that I can take my punishment for having made Absolutely No Difference; listening for anger that I'll continue to see other young people after this particular relationship is ended. But these feelings rarely emerge. Most young people seem resigned, as if it's no big deal.

It's our last session.
Aaah! Will you miss me?

Some just stop coming. A week later, they apologise in the corridor and we reschedule the appointment. But when they don't turn up for the next appointment, I start to wonder. I seek them out but they assure me (just as boyfriends and girlfriends assure each other) that they *do* want to keep meeting. We fix another appointment but, again, the same thing happens. Time passes. With young people who've effectively gone AWOL, I work hard to convene a final session, particularly when their earlier experiences in life have been of unsatisfactory endings. I want them to experience an ending where they stay in control but where the ending isn't fudged. Sometimes they come back for one final session but, even then, it's no big deal.

It's our last session.
I know and I'm really sorry but I've got to leave early.

Other young people keep coming to their appointments but do so less reliably and I wonder whether their erratic attendance has become a way of asking, 'Have I had enough? What do you think?' I wonder whether they're disappointed because I haven't made everything all right or whether a little was always enough. I tell them what I think because there are times when young people need the containment of a straight answer.

> *It's our last session.*
> *Our last? Oh yeah!*

There are sudden I-don't-think-I-need-to-come-any-more endings, which feel a bit like being jilted. Typically, on the day of our scheduled appointment, the young person finds me to tell me this. I ask questions, probing to see whether there's an avoidance of tricky stuff – disappointment, attachment, pain – because when the going gets tough some young people stop going. I ask myself whether this young person needs to know that they matter enough for me to fight for our relationship to continue. But no, 'It's okay,' they say with no particular emotional charge. At this point I can let them hold on to this most important defence – their right not to come – or shame them by the manner of my recognising some unspoken avoidance. Usually they've had enough – they're done. I smile, thank them for coming to tell me and wish them well.

> *It's our last session.*
> *I know! I won't be able to miss any more lessons!*

With some young people, we start meeting less often; with others, I allow things to change from therapy to what feels more like maintenance. There are relationships which begin with a bang, then go through a period of consolidation after which the work seems to be done. But the young person doesn't want to end and says so. Although we're no longer talking about the raw stuff, they're obviously still pleased to come and pleased that they're still deserving of someone else's time, even without a crisis.

It's our last session.
Yeah, but you said I could come back, so it's not like we're really ending.

I notice and work with oblique references to separation and loss as they occur towards the end of a counselling relationship. Aha, I think, here's an opportunity to explore other losses in this young person's life, an opportunity to confront some existential givens, an opportunity to talk more explicitly about the meaning of our own ending. And sometimes this helps. Sometimes it takes us into important areas, but there's never a formula and my predictions about the kind of ending we'll have are frequently wrong.

It's our last session.
I know. You keep saying.

So I worry that there should be more weeping and wailing and gnashing of teeth, that these underwhelming endings are really a way of *not* ending and that I'm colluding with something unhealthy, continuing a pattern. I suspect, though, that the way young people end counselling is related to the way they begin it.

Do you do counselling?
Yes.
Oh.
Would you like to fix an appointment?
Don't know really.

Sometimes they begin because of an event or because of a person who's officially to blame for how they're feeling and we talk about that. But what they're really asking for is to be accompanied during a transition with no way of knowing how long that transition will last and with no way of knowing what they'll need from this vague thing called 'counselling'.

My teacher said I should see you.
For a counselling appointment?
Don't know. She just said to come and see you.

We begin somewhere. I don't do formal assessments, first because it's not fair to turn away a young person who's summoned the courage to approach me, however slight the presenting problem may appear to be. Young people suffering in silence are just as deserving as the ones who shout the loudest and are most urgently referred, and this may be the first time that the young person has ever dared to initiate a relationship. Second, there are attachment implications (Holmes 2001) for young people trusting and telling their story to one counsellor in an assessment meeting, only to be put on a list, waiting to start all over again with another counsellor several weeks later. For some, this merely repeats the story of their lives – being passed from one adult to another. So, with most young people, I agree that we'll start meeting as soon as possible and for as long as necessary. Agreeing to a set number of sessions makes little sense. Adults can commit themselves to six sessions with some understanding of what that commitment means but young people tend to live from week to week. They'll say yes to six sessions but it'll mean nothing. Once they've had enough, they'll simply stop coming. So unless I feel that there's a particular therapeutic security to be gained by taking away a piece of paper with six or more dates scribbled on it, we end each session by arranging our next.

[Accompanied by a friend] *I'm really sorry but I've got to talk to someone because my dad's just told my mum he wants a divorce and I've got to choose who I live with and I don't know what to say!*

There's an old joke. How many psychotherapists does it take to change a light bulb? Answer – one – but the light bulb has got to want to change... I think it's a useful working assumption that young people *don't* want to change: they want *other* people to change. They're trying their best to stay the same and they're appalled by the idea that their hard-won identity might somehow be 'changed' by counselling. What I'm really doing isn't solving problems or coaxing them through a series of traditional therapeutic hoops but giving them a particular kind of space in which to think. And the manner of their ending with me will probably matter more to me (as a middle-aged person contemplating mortality) than it ever will to them.

> [In tears] *Are you the counsellor? Can I see you?*
> *Of course. What about next week?*
> *Haven't you got anything sooner?*

They have mixed feelings about the future. The immediate crisis which may have precipitated our first meeting (boyfriend or girlfriend problems or anything else) usually masks an underlying crisis of confidence, a crisis of being alone in the world, able to make choices but still reliant on other people with no one to understand what that feels like. Of course there are parents to talk about; there are good and bad experiences to assimilate, unspoken feelings to recognise. But what's on offer in counselling with young people is really a form of accompaniment which begins and usually ends tentatively.

> *So what's this 'counselling' thing?*
> *It's a chance to talk with someone about stuff that's important.*
> *Oh, right.*
> *Are you interested?*
> *Not really.*

Important things will be addressed along the way – parents *are* a mixture and so are we; anger *is* necessary; we really *will* all die; the future *is* quite daunting and cowardice is normal. A few lurking superegos may be detoxified but, more importantly, young people take from counselling an abiding sense of being interesting and understandable despite all that's happened and is still happening in their lives. And being understandable is profoundly reassuring. Holmes (2001) writes that 'Therapy begins – and ends – with finding a therapist "who understands how I feel"' (p.132).

I know you're really busy but I was wondering whether it would be possible for me to see you sometime… It doesn't matter when… It's not urgent…

The attachments young people make as teenagers are always transitional. Unconsciously they're always moving on from mother – re-interpreting her, renegotiating their relationship with her, re-evaluating her love. In that sense, their every effort with a counselling mother goes into *not* ending but being allowed to move on. They sometimes want to have a rest but not 'end' because ending means letting go and jumping off into a future which isn't half as exciting as adults pretend. In fact, it's downright scary. Adults sometimes use it as a stick with which to beat young people ('What about the future? You've got to think of the future! You've got your whole life ahead of you!') and young people are obliged to say that they're looking forward to the future when what they really mean is 'I'm not looking forward to it at all – at least, not much!' Perhaps endings in counselling with young people are necessarily unfinished in the same way that young people leave home knowing they can always come back and knowing that the goodbyes are always temporary.

Of course there are some for whom the end of counselling (like the break up of any relationship) precipitates a fresh crisis of confidence ('How will I manage? Who will understand me now? Will I be alone again? What will become of me?') but, in my experience, this happens much less often than with adults because we haven't been working the transference in the same way. We haven't been re-experiencing a mother–baby relationship in order to amend some original fault. Rather, I've been what Lomas (1987) calls an 'environment therapist', keeping a young person company, providing safe enough conditions in which that young person can move around, explore and grow. This kind of mothering will offer new possibilities and amended ways of seeing the world, for sure, but in a more low-key, everyday way.

In schools, young people are obliged to attach and re-attach to so many different teachers; they're forever ending lessons, modules, terms, years. Finding a balance between a pragmatic but necessarily therapeutic ending to school life is difficult, and yet the way young people leave school offers them another experience of how an ending might be. I've tried hard to institute more deliberate, formalised endings in schools (Luxmoore 2000) because the way in which young people leave school is at least as important as their leave-taking with a counsellor. For at least five years, 'school' has been a hugely important transference object for them (Luxmoore 2008) and some schools are hopeless at endings. Teachers claim to be too busy to organise appropriate occasions and claim that young people aren't really affected by these things anyway. Maybe I try to compensate for these institutional resistances by worrying that my own endings with young people should somehow be more decisive and cathartic.

It's our last session.
I know.
We probably won't see each other again.
Really?
Unlikely. Certainly not after you've left school.

What, never?
Well we might see each other in the street and stop and say hello.
But I won't ask you about your mum and step-dad or any of the things we've talked about here.
Right.
So this is the last time we'll meet like this.
Right...
What's that feel like?
Don't know, really. Weird!

Perhaps I'm describing the uncertainty of transitions rather than the certainty of endings. I like Phillips's (2006) description of therapy as a conversation which is never ended, only abandoned. I say goodbye to young people, telling myself that I've worked myself out of a job, that I'm now a redundant parent-figure – ordinarily imperfect. This way, I feel better about endings which haven't seemed especially momentous. Perhaps that's how they need to be.

We've got a couple of minutes left.
It feels weird thinking that I won't be coming to this room after today. Really weird.
I think you're right. It is weird.
Ah, well. [Smiles.]
We won't see each other but we'll remember each other.
Yeah, that's right! [School bell rings.] *Thanks, anyway.*
You're welcome. Take care.
I will. You take care, too. [Stands up.] *Better go to French now.*

REFERENCES

Alford, C.F. (2006) 'Kleinian Theory Is Natural Law Theory.' In J. Mills (ed.) *Other Banalities: Melanie Klein Revisited.* Hove: Routledge.

Arendt, H. (1963) *Eichmann in Jerusalem.* London: Penguin Books.

Balindt, M. (1968) *The Basic Fault.* London: Hogarth Press.

Bowlby, J. (1969, 1973, 1980) *Attachment and Loss. Volumes 1, 2 and 3.* London: Hogarth Press.

Bramley, W. (2008) *Bewitched, Bothered and Bewildered.* London: Karnac Books.

Eigen, M. (2006) 'Destruction and Madness.' In J. Mills (ed.) *Other Banalities: Melanie Klein Revisited.* Hove: Routledge.

Elias, N. and Scotson, J.L. (1994) *The Established and the Outsiders.* London: Sage.

Fairbairn, W.R.D. (1952) *Psychoanalytic Studies of the Personality.* London: Tavistock Publications.

Fonagy, P. (2004) 'The Developmental Roots of Violence in the Failure of Mentalisation.' In F. Pfafflin and G. Adshead (eds) *A Matter of Security: The Application of Attachment Theory to Forensic Psychiatry and Psychotherapy.* London: Jessica Kingsley Publishers.

Fonagy, P., Gergely, G., Jurist, E.J. and Target, M. (2004) *Affect Regulation, Mentalisation and the Development of the Self.* London: Karnac Books.

Freud, S. (1900) *The Interpretation of Dreams.* London: Hogarth Press.

Freud, S. (1914) *On Narcissism.* London: Hogarth Press.

Garland, C. (1982) 'Group-analysis: Taking the Non-problem Seriously.' In H. Behr (ed.) *Group Analysis Vol XV, No 1.* London: Institute of Group Analysis.

Gerhardt, S. (2004) *Why Love Matters.* Hove: Brunner-Routledge.

Gomez, L. (1997) *An Introduction to Object Relations.* London: Free Association Books.

Hillman, J. (1964) *Loose Ends.* Dallas, TX: Springer Publications.

Holmes, J. (2001) *The Search for the Secure Base.* Hove: Brunner-Routledge.

Kernberg, O.F. (1970) 'A psychoanalytic classification of character pathology.' *Journal of the American Psychoanalytic Association 18,* 800–822.

Kernberg, O.F. (1992) *Aggression in Personality Disorders and Perversion.* New Haven, CT, and London: Yale University Press.

Klein, M. (1975) 'Infantile Anxiety Situations Reflected in a Work of Art and in the Creative Impulse.' In *Collected Works of Melanie Klein. Vol 1.* London: Hogarth Press and Institute of Psychoanalysis. (Original work published 1929)

REFERENCES

Klein, M. (1975) 'A Contribution to the Psychogenesis of Manic-depressive States.' In *Collected Works of Melanie Klein. Vol 1.* London: Hogarth Press and Institute of Psychoanalysis. (Original work published 1935)

Klein, M. (1957) *Envy and Gratitude: A Study of Unconscious Sources.* London: Tavistock Publications.

Kohut, H. (1971) *The Analysis of the Self.* New York, NY: International Universities Press.

Lomas, P. (1973) *True and False Experience.* London: Allen Lane.

Lomas, P. (1987) *The Limits of Interpretation.* London: Constable & Robinson.

Luxmoore, N. (2000) *Listening to Young People in School, Youth Work and Counselling.* London: Jessica Kingsley Publishers.

Luxmoore, N. (2006) *Working with Anger and Young People.* London: Jessica Kingsley Publishers.

Luxmoore, N. (2008) *Feeling Like Crap: Young People and the Meaning of Self-esteem.* London: Jessica Kingsley Publishers.

Mann, D. (2002) 'In Search of Love and Hate.' In D. Mann (ed.) *Love and Hate: Psychoanalytic Perspectives.* Hove: Brunner-Routledge.

McGuire, W. (ed.) (1974) *The Freud/Jung Letters: The Correspondence Between Sigmund Freud and C.G. Jung.* Princeton, NJ: Princeton University Press.

Mollon, P. (2001) *Releasing the Self: The Healing Legacy of Heinz Kohut.* London: Whurr Publishers.

Nussbaum, M.C. (2001) *Upheavals of Thought.* Cambridge: Cambridge University Press.

Phillips, A. (2006) *Side Effects.* London: Hamish Hamilton.

Savage, J. (2007) *Teenage: The Creation of Youth 1875–1945.* London: Chatto and Windus.

Shriver, L. (2005) *We Need to Talk about Kevin.* London: Serpent's Tail.

Spinelli, E. (2001) *The Mirror and the Hammer.* London: Continuum Books.

Suttie, I.D. (1935) *The Origins of Love and Hate.* London: Kegan Paul.

Symington, N. (1993) *Narcissism: A New Theory.* London: Karnac Books.

Winnicott, D.W. (1958) 'Hate in the Countertransference.' In D.W. Winnicott *Through Paediatrics to Psychoanalysis: Collected Papers.* London: Tavistock Publications. (Original work published 1947)

Winnicott, D.W. (1958) *Through Paediatrics to Psychoanalysis: Collected Papers.* London: Tavistock Publications.

Winnicott, D.W. (1965) *The Maturational Processes and the Facilitating Environment.* London: Hogarth Press.

Winnicott, D.W. (1971) *Playing and Reality.* London: Routledge.

Zeki, S. and Romaya, J.P. (2008) *Neural Correlates of Hate.* PLoS ONE 3(10): e3556. doi:10.1371/journal.pone.0003556

INDEX